SALARIYA

**WARNING: Fixatives should be
used only under adult supervision.**

Published in Great Britain in MMXIII by
Book House, an imprint of
The Salariya Book Company Ltd
25 Marlborough Place, Brighton BN1 1UB

1 3 5 7 9 8 6 4 2

Please visit our website at **www.salariya.com**
for **free** electronic versions of:
You Wouldn't Want to Be an Egyptian Mummy!
You Wouldn't Want to Be a Roman Gladiator!
You Wouldn't Want to be a Polar Explorer!
You Wouldn't Want to sail on a 19th-Century Whaling Ship!

Authors:
Mark Bergin was born in Hastings, England, in 1961.
He studied at Eastbourne College of Art and has
specialised in historical reconstructions as well as aviation
and maritime subjects since 1983. He lives in
Bexhill-on-Sea with his wife and three children.

David Antram was born in Brighton, England, in 1958.
He studied at Eastbourne College of Art and then worked in
advertising for fifteen years before becoming a full-time artist.
He has illustrated many children's non-fiction books.

Carolyn Franklin is a graduate of Brighton College of Art, England,
specialising in design and illustration. She has worked in animation,
advertising and children's fiction and non-fiction. She has a particular interest
in natural history and has written and illustrated many books on the subject.

Editor: Rob Walker

PB ISBN: 978-1-908759-69-6

PAPER FROM
SUSTAINABLE
FORESTS

A CIP catalogue record for this
book is available from the
British Library.

Printed and bound in China.
Printed on paper from sustainable sources.

You
Tube

FIND OUR BOOKS
ON THE APP STORE:
SEARCH FOR 'SALARIYA'

@bookhousebooks   The Salariya   BookHouse100
                   Book Company

Visit our **new** online shop at
shop.salariya.com
for great offers, gift ideas, all our new releas
and free postage and packaging.

DRAW
SCARY CREATURES

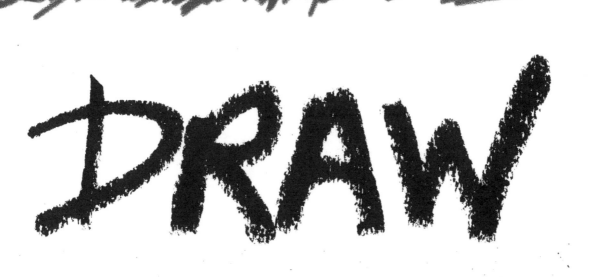

BOOK  HOUSE

Contents

DRAW

Drawing materials

Try using different types of drawing papers and materials. Experiment with charcoal, wax crayons and pastels. All pens, from felt-tips to ballpoints, will make interesting marks — try drawing with pen and ink on wet paper for a variety of results.

Silhouette is a style of drawing that uses only a solid black shape.

Ink

Charcoal is very soft and can be used for big, bold drawings. Ask an adult to spray your charcoal drawings with fixative to prevent smudging.

You can create special effects in a drawing done with **wax crayons** by scraping parts of the colour away.

Felt-tip

Felt-tips come in a range of line widths. The wider pens are good for filling in large areas of flat tone.

6

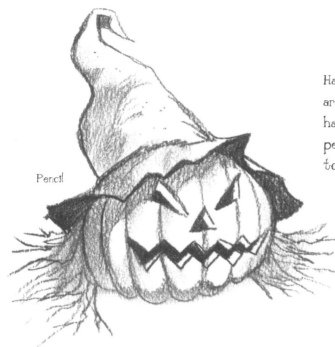

Pencil

Hard **pencil** leads are greyer and soft pencil leads are blacker. Hard pencils are graded from 6H (the hardest) through 5H, 4H, 3H and 2H to H. Soft pencils are graded from B, 2B, 3B, 4B and 5B up to 6B (the softest).

Pastels are even softer than charcoal, and come in a wide range of colours. Ask an adult to spray your pastel drawings with fixative to prevent smudging.

Lines drawn in **ink** cannot be erased, so keep your ink drawings sketchy and less rigid. Don't worry about mistakes as these lines can be lost in the drawing as it develops.

Perspective

DRAW

If you look at any object from different viewpoints, you will see that the part that is closest to you will look larger, and the part furthest away from you will look smaller. Drawing in perspective is a way of creating a feeling of space — of showing three dimensions on a flat surface.

Box construction lines can help with perspective.

The vanishing point (V.P.) is the place in a perspective drawing where parallel lines appear to meet. The position of the vanishing point depends on the viewer's eye level. Sometimes a low viewpoint can give your drawing added drama.

V.P.

Two-point perspective drawing

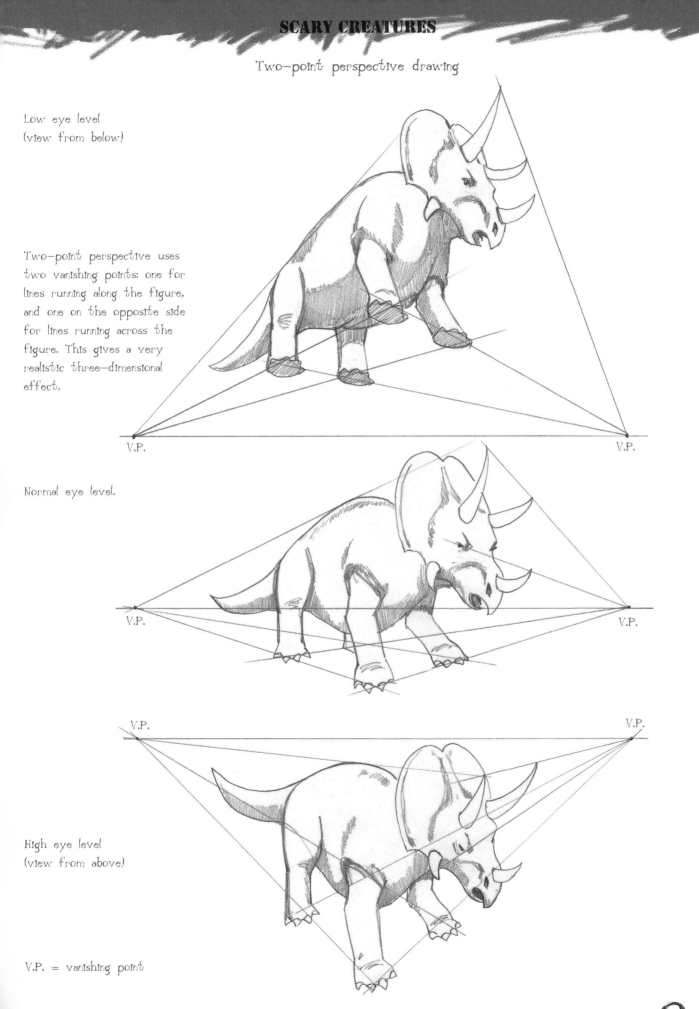

Low eye level
(view from below)

Two-point perspective uses two vanishing points: one for lines running along the figure, and one on the opposite side for lines running across the figure. This gives a very realistic three-dimensional effect.

V.P.   V.P.

Normal eye level.

V.P.   V.P.

V.P.   V.P.

High eye level
(view from above)

V.P. = vanishing point

9

Sleeping DRAW dragon

A dragon sleeping peacefully in its den makes for a very interesting composition.

Draw two curved lines for the neck.

Start by drawing a large oval for the body.

Draw a circle for the head.

Draw simple shapes for the legs.

Draw a long curved line to indicate the dragon's spine and tail.

Draw the basic shape of the face using straight lines.

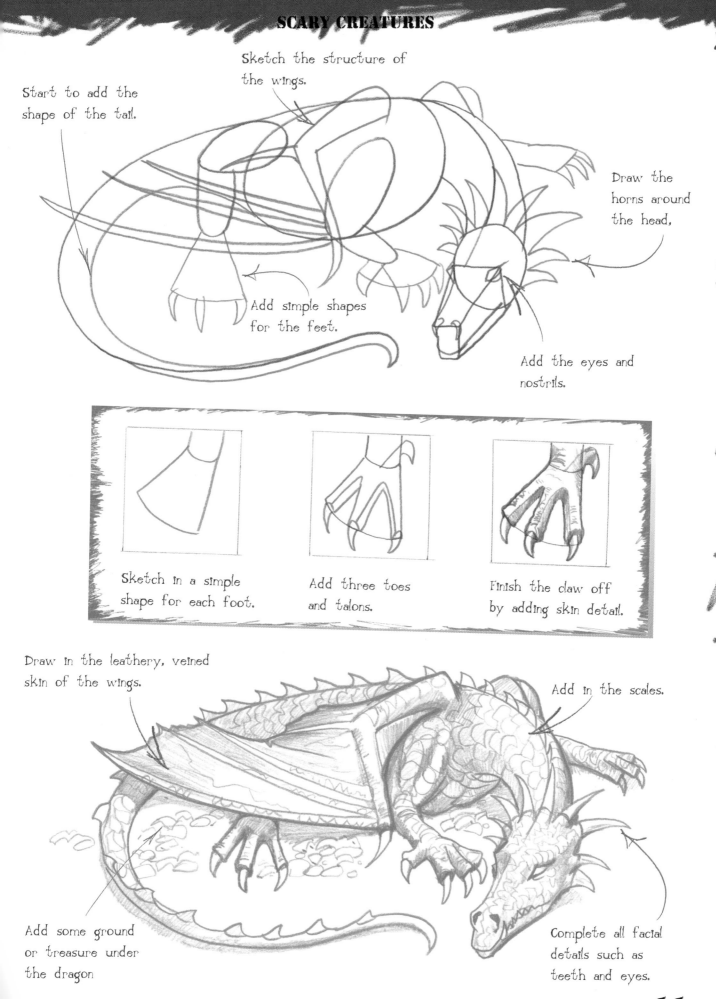

Sketch the structure of
the wings.

Start to add the
shape of the tail.

Draw the
horns around
the head,

Add simple shapes
for the feet.

Add the eyes and
nostrils.

Sketch in a simple
shape for each foot.

Add three toes
and talons.

Finish the claw off
by adding skin detail.

Draw in the leathery, veined
skin of the wings.

Add in the scales.

Add some ground
or treasure under
the dragon

Complete all facial
details such as
teeth and eyes.

11

DRAW Fire-breathing dragon

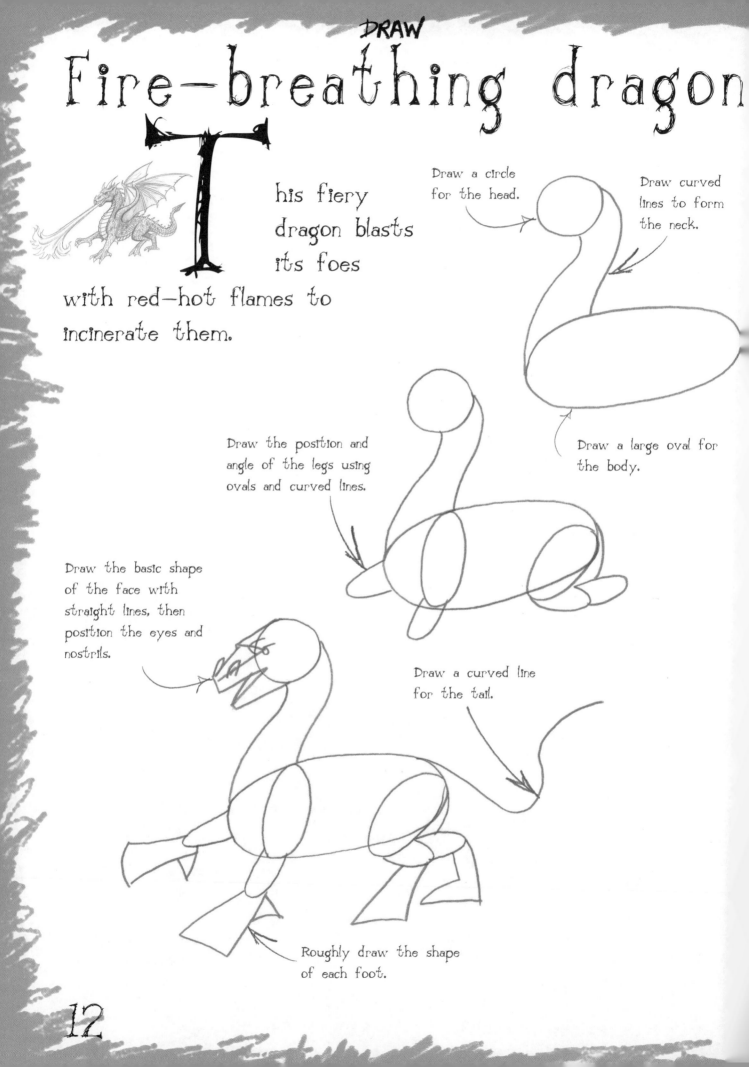

This fiery dragon blasts its foes with red-hot flames to incinerate them.

Draw a circle for the head.

Draw curved lines to form the neck.

Draw a large oval for the body.

Draw the position and angle of the legs using ovals and curved lines.

Draw the basic shape of the face with straight lines, then position the eyes and nostrils.

Draw a curved line for the tail.

Roughly draw the shape of each foot.

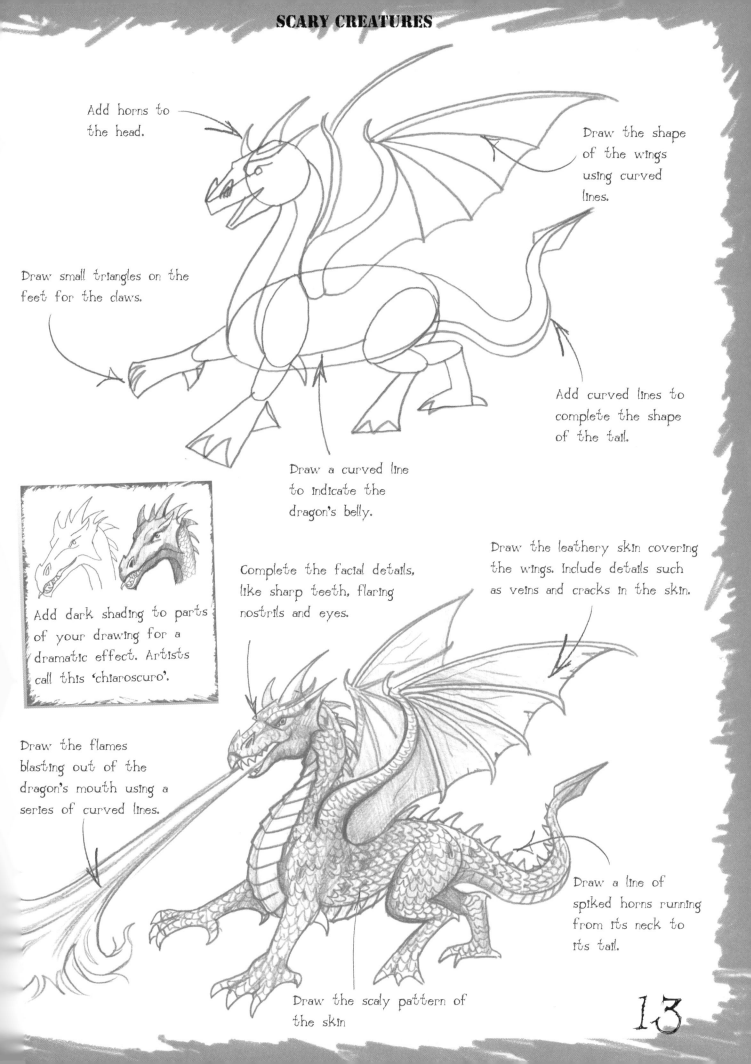

Add horns to the head.

Draw the shape of the wings using curved lines.

Draw small triangles on the feet for the claws.

Add curved lines to complete the shape of the tail.

Draw a curved line to indicate the dragon's belly.

Add dark shading to parts of your drawing for a dramatic effect. Artists call this 'chiaroscuro'.

Complete the facial details, like sharp teeth, flaring nostrils and eyes.

Draw the leathery skin covering the wings. Include details such as veins and cracks in the skin.

Draw the flames blasting out of the dragon's mouth using a series of curved lines.

Draw a line of spiked horns running from its neck to its tail.

Draw the scaly pattern of the skin

13

Perched dragon

This dragon is perched on a large rock waiting patiently for its next victim to appear.

Draw a circle for the head.

Draw two curved lines for the neck.

Draw a large oval for the body.

Draw in the basic shape of the head.

Draw a curved horn shape for the arm of the wing.

Add two overlapped ovals for the rear leg.

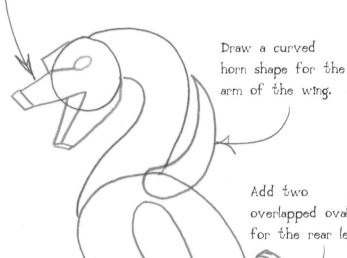

Draw in the front legs using simple shapes.

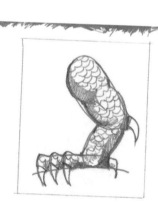

Remember when drawing the dragon's legs that shading helps define the muscle.

14

Add horns to
the head.

Draw in a curved line
for the tongue.

Draw a line to
indicate the belly.

Add on the feet
and claws.

Draw curved lines
for the shape of
the wings.

Add details of the dragon's
head, remembering the sharp
teeth and pointed tongue.

Draw two long lines
coming to a point for
the tail.

Draw the leathery veined
skin of the wings. Add
interesting details like
tears and holes.

Draw the rock the dragon
is perched on.

15

Flying dragon

DRAW

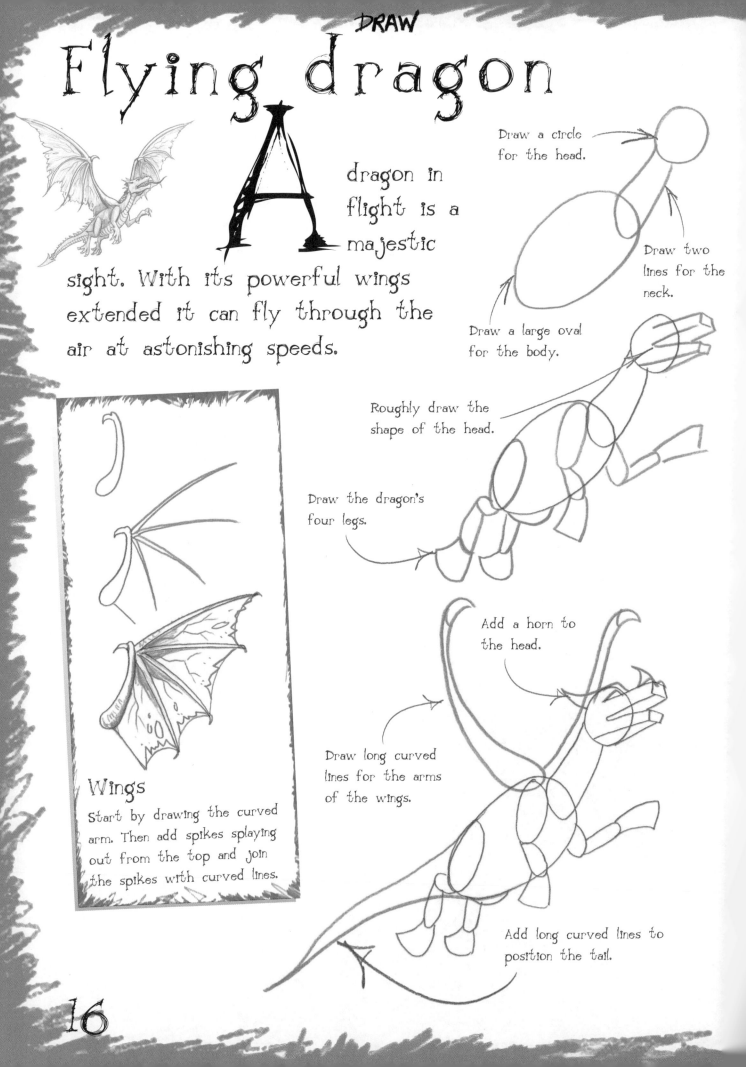

A dragon in flight is a majestic sight. With its powerful wings extended it can fly through the air at astonishing speeds.

Draw a circle for the head.

Draw two lines for the neck.

Draw a large oval for the body.

Roughly draw the shape of the head.

Draw the dragon's four legs.

Add a horn to the head.

Draw long curved lines for the arms of the wings.

Add long curved lines to position the tail.

Wings

Start by drawing the curved arm. Then add spikes splaying out from the top and join the spikes with curved lines.

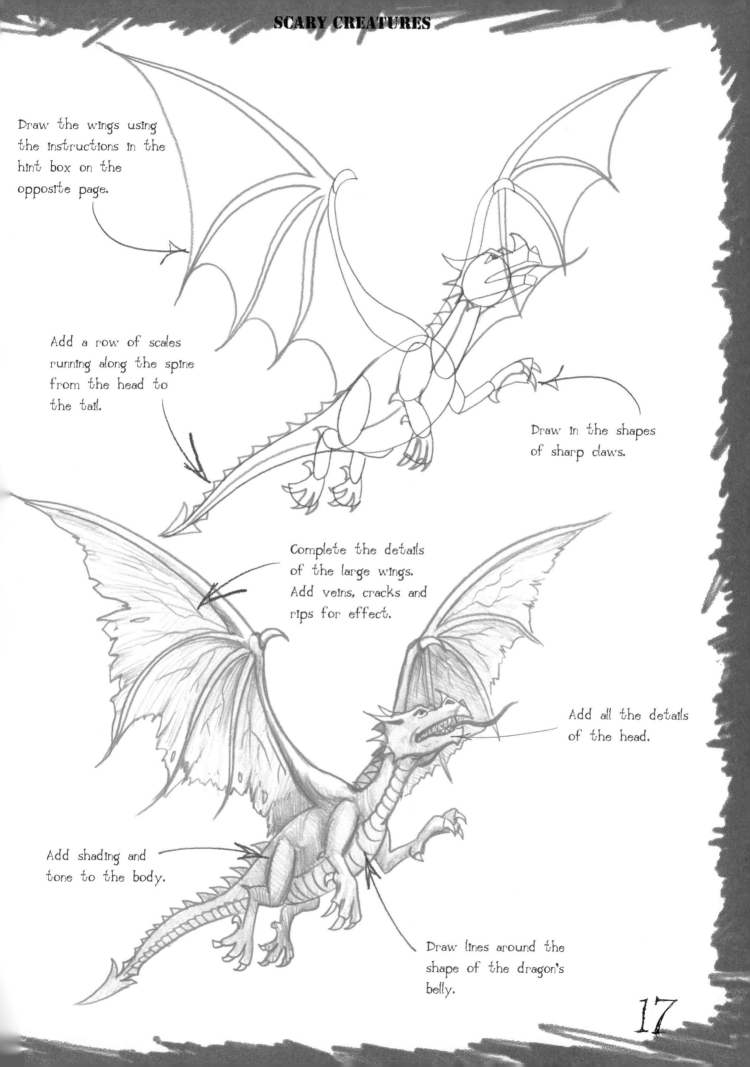

Draw the wings using the instructions in the hint box on the opposite page.

Add a row of scales running along the spine from the head to the tail.

Draw in the shapes of sharp claws.

Complete the details of the large wings. Add veins, cracks and rips for effect.

Add all the details of the head.

Add shading and tone to the body.

Draw lines around the shape of the dragon's belly.

17

Battling dragons
DRAW

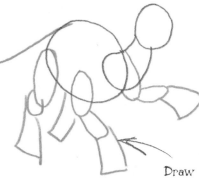

Two dragons confront one another to do battle in the sky. Who will be the winner in this ferocious fight?

Draw two circles to position the dragons' heads.

Start by drawing two large ovals for the dragons' bodies.

Add long curved lines to each dragon to position the tails.

Draw each dragon's legs, sketching in their shape simply.

Construction lines should always be drawn lightly. That way you can easily erase them when you finish the drawing.

18

Add the wing shapes to both dragons.

Draw the horns and mouths.

Draw a second curved line and add a triangle to complete the shape of the tail.

Draw fire belching from the dragon's mouth.

Sharp spikes, scales and claws make the dragon look terrifying.

Add details such as claws and scales running down the spine.

Add shading to areas that are obscure or shaded from light.

19

Fire and ice dragons

An intense battle rages in the sky! Two opposing dragons fight above a backdrop of mountains and a solar eclipse.

Draw a circle for each dragon's head and a large oval for each of their bodies.

Add a long curved line for each dragon's tail.

Join the heads to the bodies with curved lines for each dragon's neck.

Roughly sketch the shape of each head.

Draw the position and angle of each of the feet.

Add the leg shapes using ovals.

Draw the basic
structure of the wings.

Add details and
horns to both heads.

Indicate the
dragon's belly with
a curved line.

Add pointed crests
running the length of
the spine and tail.

Start adding
the shape of
the claws.

Finish off the dragon's
wings by adding tone
and battle scars.

Complete the details
of the dragons' heads.

Draw flames coming out
of one dragon's mouth.

Complete the scales
on the underside or
belly of the dragon.

Add a dramatic
background of
mountains and a
blacked-out sun.

21

DRAW Woolly rhino

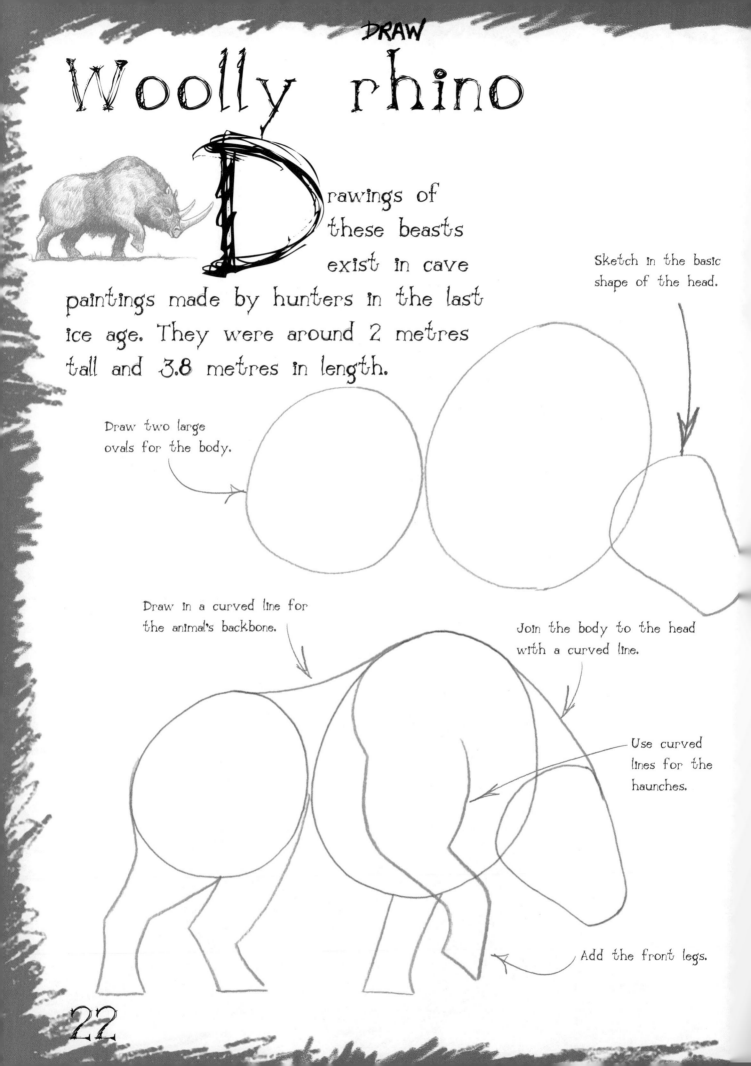

Drawings of these beasts exist in cave paintings made by hunters in the last ice age. They were around 2 metres tall and 3.8 metres in length.

Sketch in the basic shape of the head.

Draw two large ovals for the body.

Draw in a curved line for the animal's backbone.

Join the body to the head with a curved line.

Use curved lines for the haunches.

Add the front legs.

22

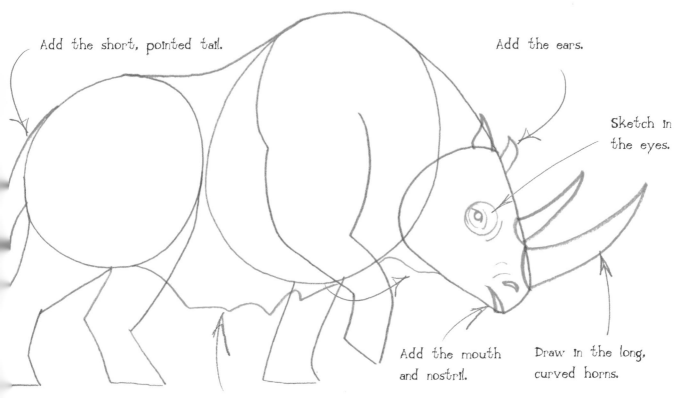

Add the short, pointed tail.

Add the ears.

Sketch in the eyes.

Add the mouth and nostril.

Draw in the long, curved horns.

Draw a jagged shape to indicate the woolly underbelly.

Draw the woolly coat using lots of short lines. Make the lines denser where you want to show shade and tone.

Add dense fur lines along the spine.

Complete the head details. Note how the fur direction changes. Add dark areas to the eye, mouth and nostril.

Sketch in coarse fur on the underbelly.

Add shading to the underside of the horns.

Add the ground.

Add darker tone to areas light wouldn't reach.

Remove any unwanted construction lines.

23

DRAW
Andrewsarchus

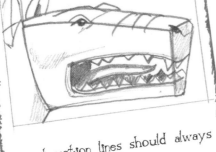

The Andrewsarchus was perhaps the largest carnivore mammal ever to live. It stood around 1.8 metres tall and was about 5.2 metres long.

Construction lines should always be drawn lightly. That way you can easily erase them when you finish the drawing.

Draw a curved line for the spine.

Start by sketching in two ovals of different sizes for the front and rear haunches.

Draw in construction lines to position the head.

Add the simple shapes for the front legs. One leg should bend.

Add the back legs. Use curved lines for the upper part.

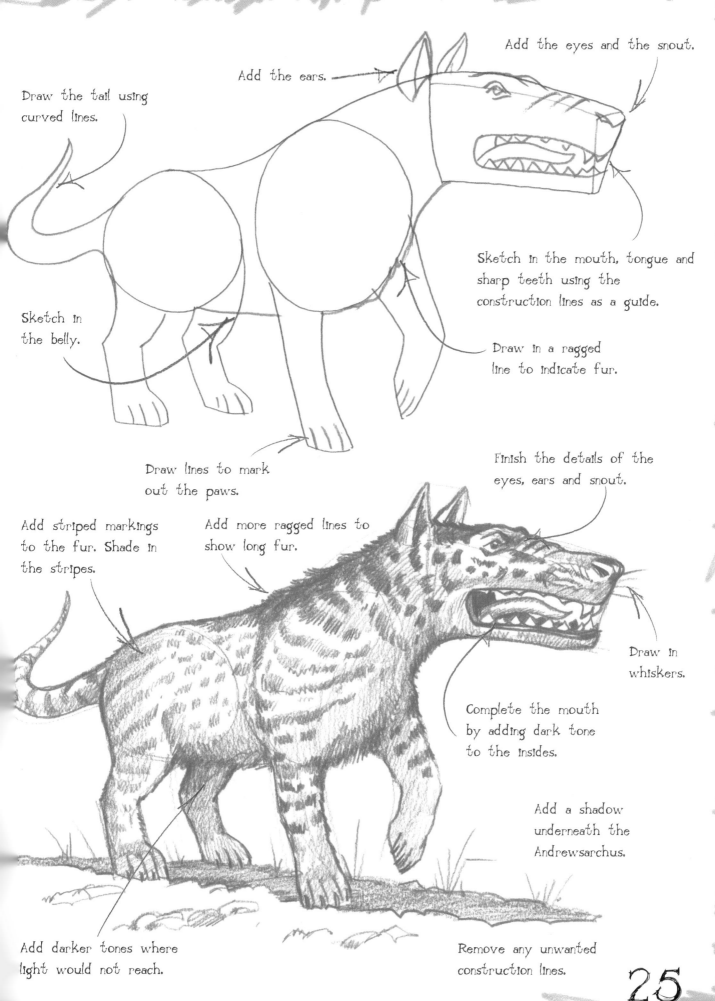

Add the eyes and the snout.

Add the ears.

Draw the tail using curved lines.

Sketch in the mouth, tongue and sharp teeth using the construction lines as a guide.

Sketch in the belly.

Draw in a ragged line to indicate fur.

Draw lines to mark out the paws.

Finish the details of the eyes, ears and snout.

Add striped markings to the fur. Shade in the stripes.

Add more ragged lines to show long fur.

Draw in whiskers.

Complete the mouth by adding dark tone to the insides.

Add a shadow underneath the Andrewsarchus.

Add darker tones where light would not reach.

Remove any unwanted construction lines.

25

Basilosaurus

The Basilosaurus was a **gigantic** carnivorous whale—like creature. Fossils of this giant creature, measuring 18 metres in length, have been found in Louisiana, Egypt and the Sahara desert.

Add an oval for the head.

Start by drawing a large bean shape for the body.

Add curvy triangular tail fins.

Draw in the tail using long curved lines.

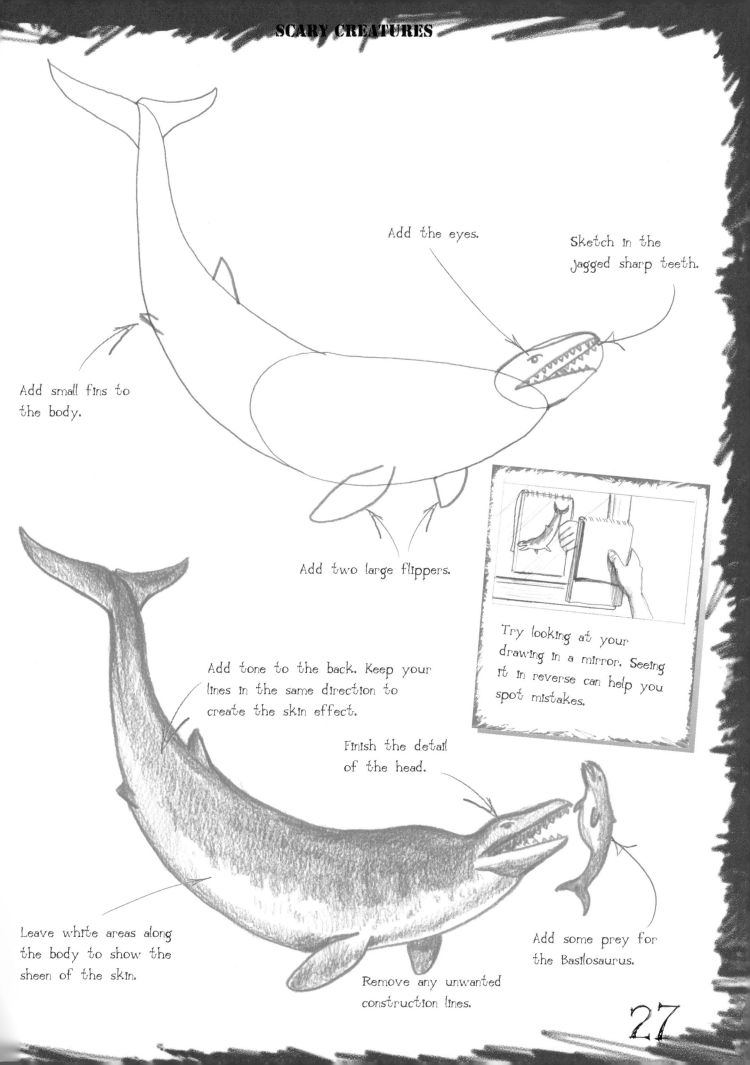

Add the eyes.

Sketch in the jagged sharp teeth.

Add small fins to the body.

Add two large flippers.

Try looking at your drawing in a mirror. Seeing it in reverse can help you spot mistakes.

Add tone to the back. Keep your lines in the same direction to create the skin effect.

Finish the detail of the head.

Leave white areas along the body to show the sheen of the skin.

Add some prey for the Basilosaurus.

Remove any unwanted construction lines.

DRAW Indricotherium

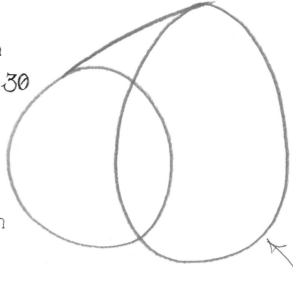

ndricotherium lived around 30 to 25 million years ago. This large land mammal would have eaten the tallest parts of trees in the same way as a giraffe.

Draw two large ovals for the body. Add a line at the top for the spine.

Draw in the thick back legs.

Add a curved underbelly.

Draw in the front legs, overlapping them to indicate one leg is behind the other.

Add two long
curved lines for
the thick neck.

Sketch in the eyes,
nose and ears.

Use curving lines to show
the shape of the head.

Draw in curved lines around the
body to suggest muscle structure.

Draw in small semicircles
for the toes.

Add tone to define the
shape of the head.

Add a long
curvy tail.

Add lots of lines to
indicate the leathery skin
folds of the body.

Add bristles at the
end of the tail.

Shade in areas where
light wouldn't reach.

Remove any
unwanted
construction lines.

Add in the ground.

DRAW
Phorusrhacos

Phorusrhacos is known as one of the 'terror birds'. It stood 3 metres tall and fed on small mammals and carcasses.

Draw an oval for the head.

Draw a curved line for the neck.

Draw a larger oval for the body.

Add a second curved line for the neck.

Sketch in the basic shape of the tail.

Draw in the legs with long curved lines.

By framing your drawing with a square or a rectangle you can make it look completely different.

Add construction lines to position the base of the feet.

Sketch in the shape of the curving beak and position the eye.

Sketch in construction lines for the head plumage.

Using the construction lines as a guide, draw in the feather shapes of the head plumage.

Add another line to the neck.

Add a jagged line for where the feathers overlap the leg.

Add lots of curved lines for the feathers.

Add tone to the beak and finish the head details.

Add toes and talons to the feet.

Shade areas where light wouldn't reach.

Sketch tonal stripes onto the legs.

Add lines to create skin texture.

Add the ground.

Remove any unwanted construction lines.

31

DRAW Megatherium

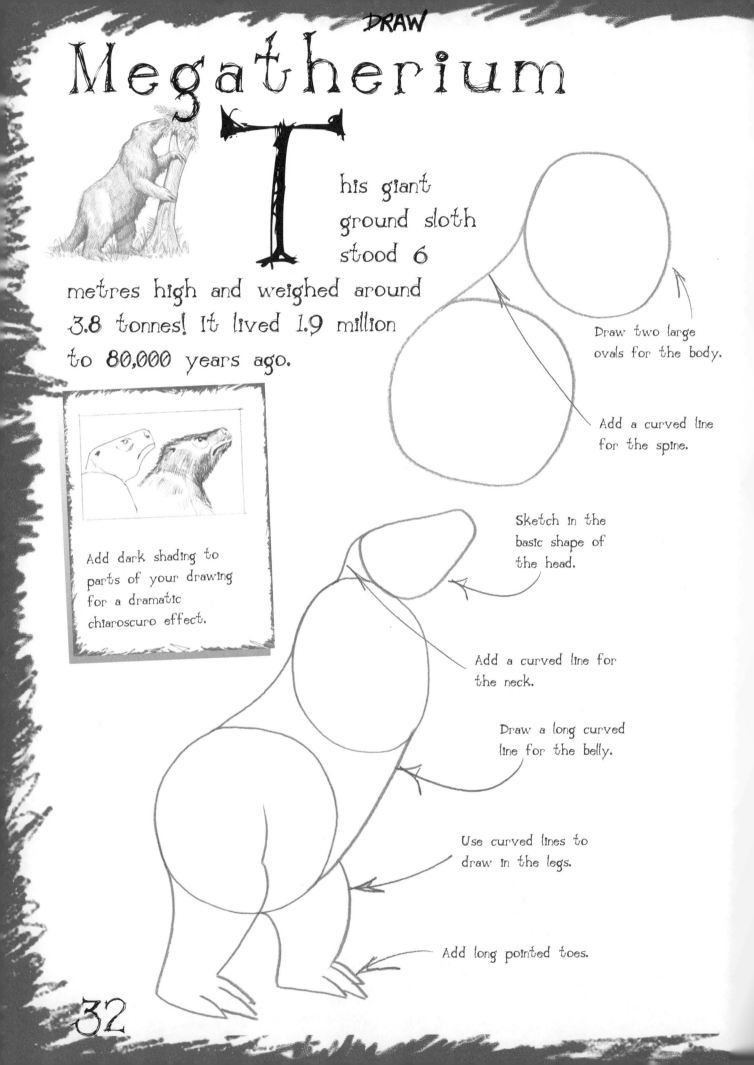

This giant ground sloth stood 6 metres high and weighed around 3.8 tonnes! It lived 1.9 million to 80,000 years ago.

Add dark shading to parts of your drawing for a dramatic chiaroscuro effect.

Draw two large ovals for the body.

Add a curved line for the spine.

Sketch in the basic shape of the head.

Add a curved line for the neck.

Draw a long curved line for the belly.

Use curved lines to draw in the legs.

Add long pointed toes.

Add the eye, nostril, ear and downturned mouth.

Sketch a jagged line around the outline to indicate fur.

Sketch in the arms with long pointed fingers.

Finish drawing the head details.

Draw in the fur using lots of short lines. Vary the frequency for areas of light and dark.

Sketch in a curved tail.

Use many short lines to define the arms.

Draw in a tree and shrubbery for added effect.

Add shading to where light won't reach.

Remove any unwanted construction lines.

33

DRAW Smilodon

This large sabre—tooth cat hunted grazing animals, pinned them down with its powerful front legs and killed them with its bite. Males could reach 3 metres in length.

Start by drawing two ovals.

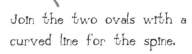

Join the two ovals with a curved line for the spine.

Add two curved lines for the neck to join the head to the body.

Always check the negative space — the areas around and between the parts of your drawing. This can help you spot mistakes.

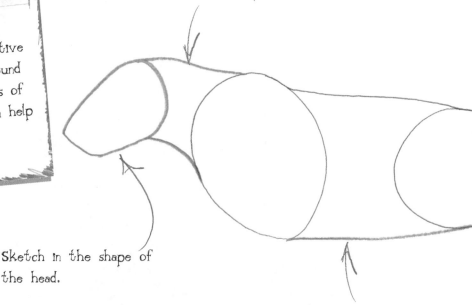

Sketch in the shape of the head.

Add a line for the belly.

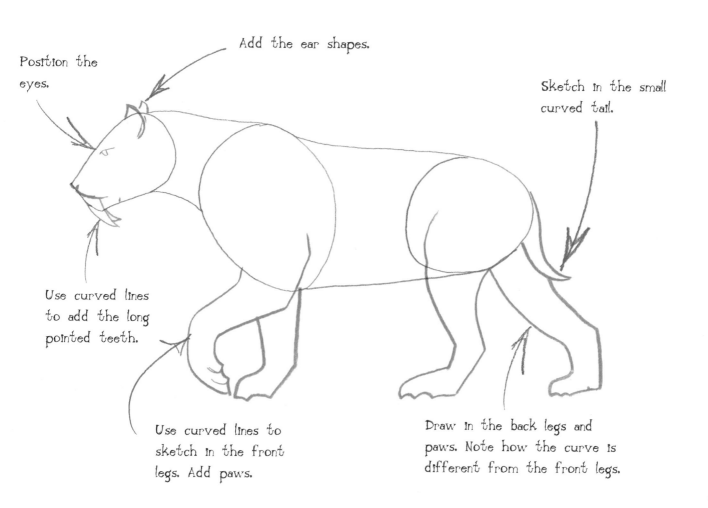

Position the eyes.

Add the ear shapes.

Sketch in the small curved tail.

Use curved lines to add the long pointed teeth.

Use curved lines to sketch in the front legs. Add paws.

Draw in the back legs and paws. Note how the curve is different from the front legs.

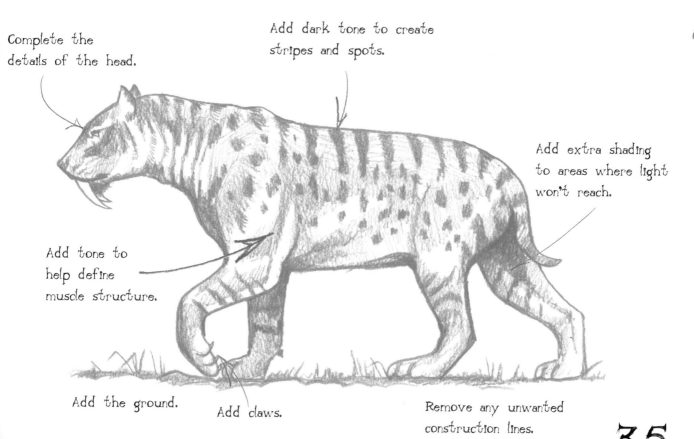

Complete the details of the head.

Add dark tone to create stripes and spots.

Add extra shading to areas where light won't reach.

Add tone to help define muscle structure.

Add the ground.

Add claws.

Remove any unwanted construction lines.

35

Attack!

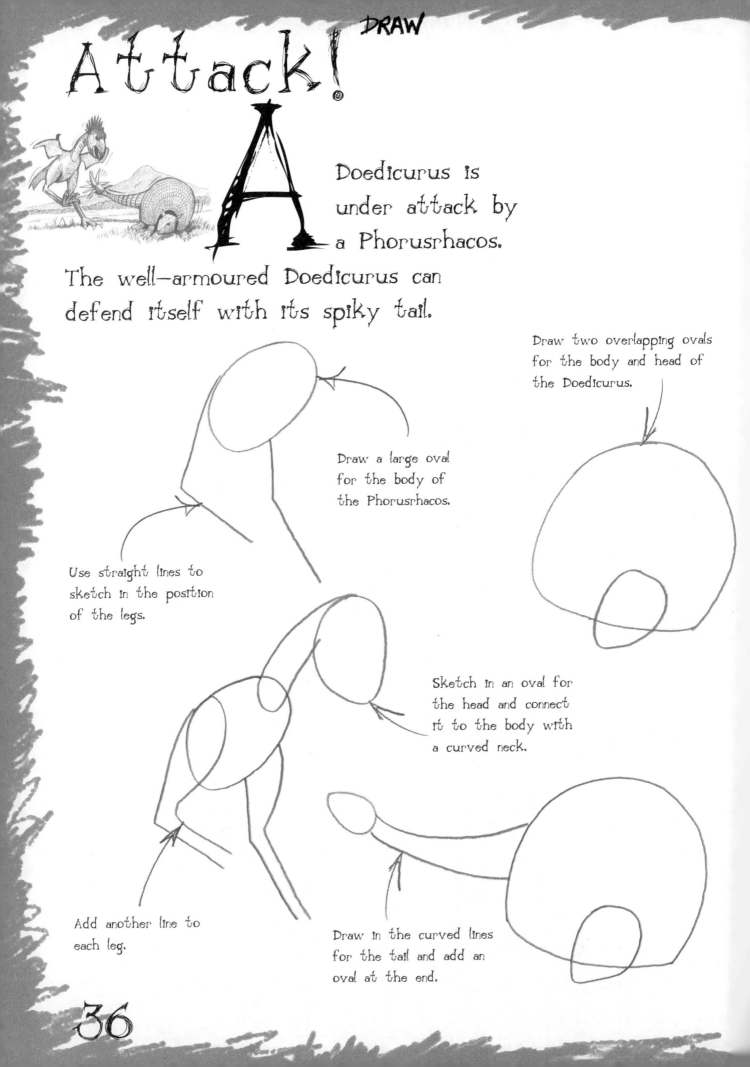

A Doedicurus is under attack by a Phorusrhacos. The well-armoured Doedicurus can defend itself with its spiky tail.

Draw two overlapping ovals for the body and head of the Doedicurus.

Draw a large oval for the body of the Phorusrhacos.

Use straight lines to sketch in the position of the legs.

Sketch in an oval for the head and connect it to the body with a curved neck.

Add another line to each leg.

Draw in the curved lines for the tail and add an oval at the end.

Draw the basic shape for the wings.

Sketch in the head plumage.

Add the eye and beak.

Position the eyes, ears and mouth.

Draw on the tail spikes.

Sketch in the tail shape.

Add armoured bands to the tail.

Draw in the three-toed claws.

Add the legs with three spiked toes.

Add areas of tone to define the body shapes.

Complete the details of the Phorusrhacos.

Draw many small ovals around the body to create the armoured exterior.

Remove any unwanted construction lines.

Draw in a background for added drama.

37

Vampire

DRAW

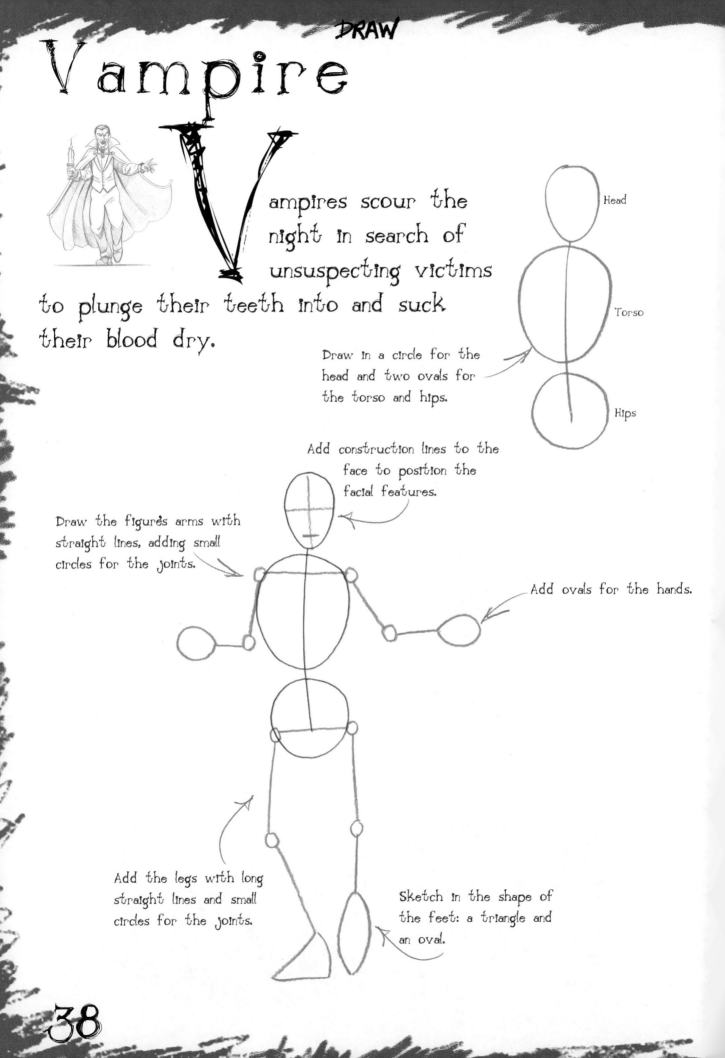

Vampires scour the night in search of unsuspecting victims to plunge their teeth into and suck their blood dry.

Draw in a circle for the head and two ovals for the torso and hips.

Head

Torso

Hips

Add construction lines to the face to position the facial features.

Draw the figure's arms with straight lines, adding small circles for the joints.

Add ovals for the hands.

Add the legs with long straight lines and small circles for the joints.

Sketch in the shape of the feet: a triangle and an oval.

raw a simple candle in
he vampire's hand.

Sketch in the facial features using the
construction lines as a guide. Add the
V-shaped hairline.

Add fingers to the oval hand.

Sketch in the shirt,
adding cuffs and collar.

Draw the cape and
collar using flowing
curved lines.

Add the
waistcoat and
trousers with
simple lines.

Complete the details of the
face. Add tone to the hair
and the mouth.

Draw in the chain
using circles.

Add details to the candle
and hands.

Add shading to areas
light wouldn't reach.

Add buttons
and details to
the waistcoat.

Draw long curved lines
for folds in the cape.

Finish the detail
on the shoes.

Use an eraser to remove any unwanted construction lines.

Zombie

The dead have risen and are walking the earth! The zombies will not stop until they have killed you and made you one of their own.

Sketch in basic construction lines to place facial features.

Head

Torso

Hips

Draw an oval for the head and two circles for the torso and hips. Join these with a centre line.

Add circles for the neck, shoulders and elbows.

Sketch in ovals for the hands.

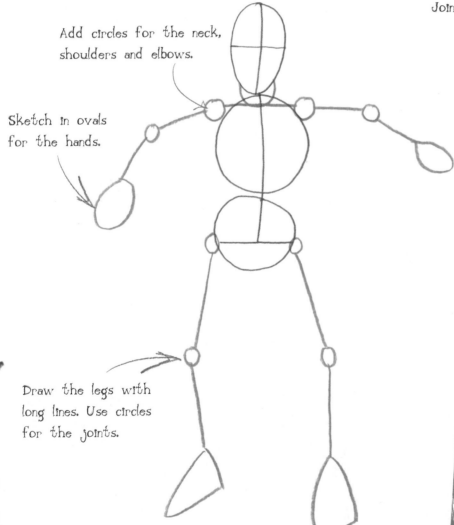

Draw the legs with long lines. Use circles for the joints.

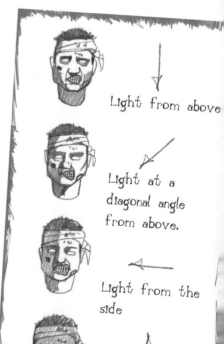

Light from above

Light at a diagonal angle from above.

Light from the side

Light from below

Changing the direction of the light source in a drawing can create drama and mood.

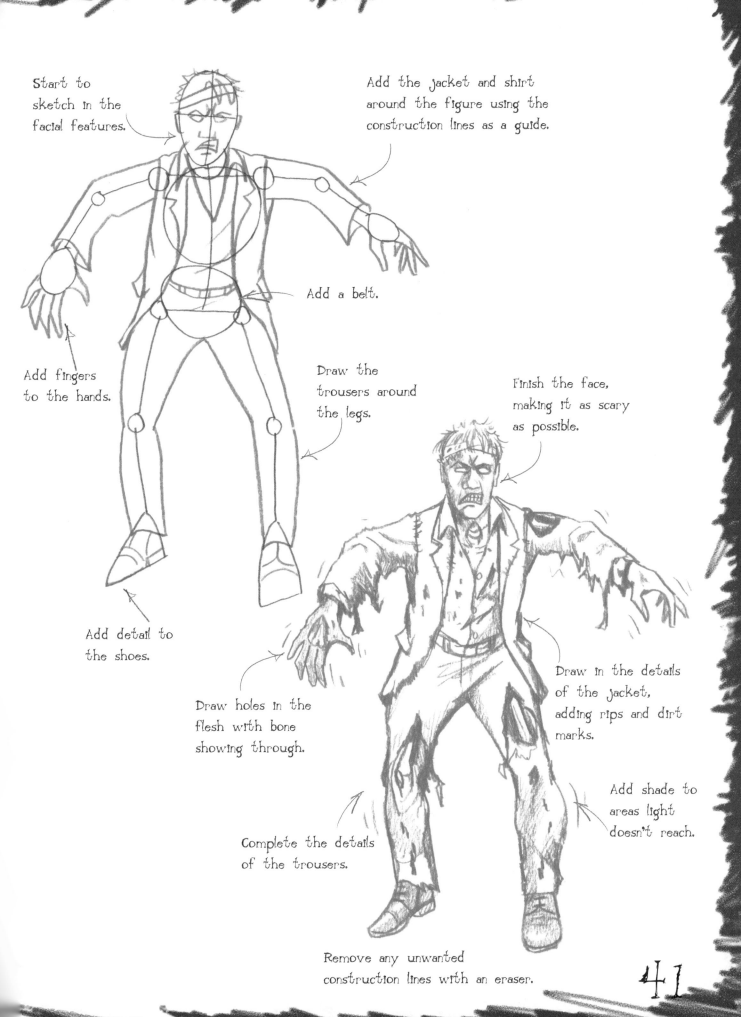

Start to sketch in the facial features.

Add the jacket and shirt around the figure using the construction lines as a guide.

Add a belt.

Add fingers to the hands.

Draw the trousers around the legs.

Finish the face, making it as scary as possible.

Add detail to the shoes.

Draw holes in the flesh with bone showing through.

Draw in the details of the jacket, adding rips and dirt marks.

Add shade to areas light doesn't reach.

Complete the details of the trousers.

Remove any unwanted construction lines with an eraser.

41

Ghoul

Ghouls haunt graveyards or any other place that dead human flesh can be found. They devour the rotting meat, leaving nothing but the bones.

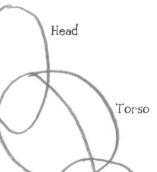

Draw a long oval for the head.

Head

Torso

Draw circles for the torso and hips.

Draw a curved line for the bent spine.

Add construction lines to the head to place the facial features.

Position the arms using lines and circles for the joints.

Sketch in ovals for the hands.

Add long lines for the legs and circles for the joints.

Draw in the creature's large feet.

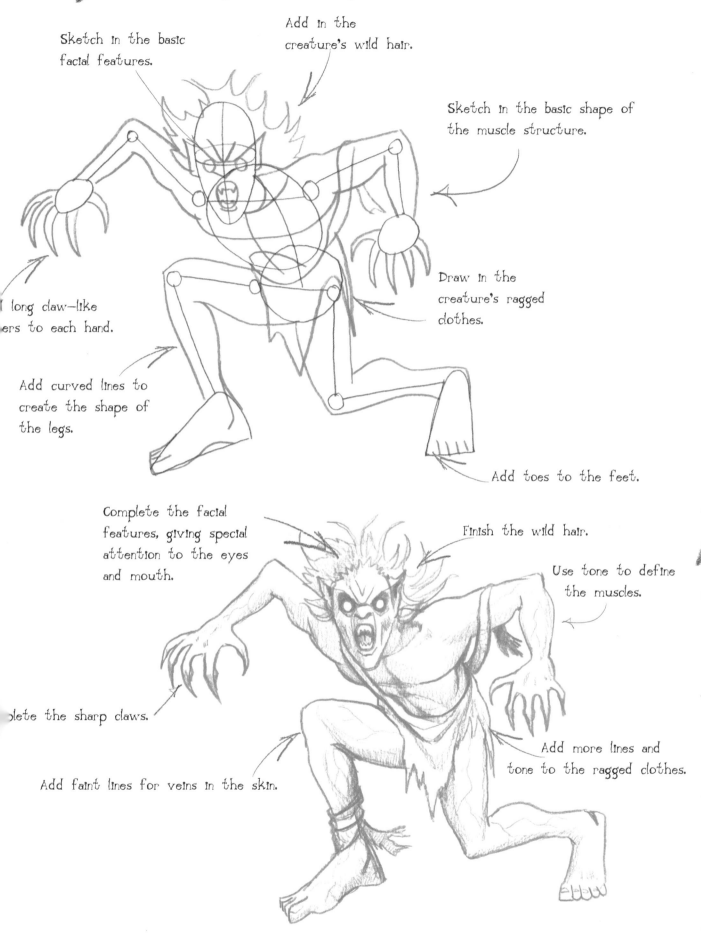

Sketch in the basic facial features.

Add in the creature's wild hair.

Sketch in the basic shape of the muscle structure.

long claw—like ers to each hand.

Draw in the creature's ragged clothes.

Add curved lines to create the shape of the legs.

Add toes to the feet.

Complete the facial features, giving special attention to the eyes and mouth.

Finish the wild hair.

Use tone to define the muscles.

lete the sharp claws.

Add more lines and tone to the ragged clothes.

Add faint lines for veins in the skin.

Use an eraser to remove any unwanted construction lines.

43

Werewolf DRAW

Beware the full moon! Once this lunar phase is entered, these unassuming cursed people transform into creatures that are halfman and halfwolf, and will tear their victims apart!

Head

Torso

Hips

Sketch an oval for the head and two circles for the torso and hips. Add a centre line for the spine and a line for the hips.

Add lines for the arms with circles for the joints.

Add circles for the hands.

Draw short lines for the legs.

Draw circles to indicate joints.

Add two large flipper-like feet.

44

Position the ear and eye.

Sketch in construction lines for the shape of the snout.

Add claws to the hands.

Join the head to the shoulders.

Finish the snout details and add sharp teeth.

Sketch in the ripped trousers.

Draw in the limbs using the construction lines as a guide.

Draw lots of short lines to indicate the fur.

Join the torso to the hips

Add the shape of the tail.

Complete the hands, adding pads and claws.

Add claws to the feet.

Finish the furry tail.

Complete the torn and ragged trousers.

Remove any unwanted construction lines with an eraser.

Draw in the details of the elongated feet.

45

Ghost

Ghosts are the souls of the 'dead' who cannot rest. They haunt people at night, filling them with terror.

Head

Torso

Hips

Sketch three ovals for the head, torso and hips. Join these with a centre line for the spine.

Sketch a construction line to place the eyes.

Add lines for the arms with circles for the joints.

Add ovals for the hands.

Add long lines for the legs with circles for the joints.

Sketch in basic shapes for the feet.

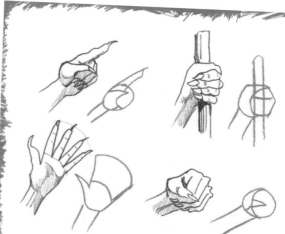

Drawing hands
Practise sketching your own hands in different positions. This will help you draw characters with expressive hands.

Add pointed fingers.

Sketch in the arms using the construction lines as a guide.

Draw dark holes for the eyes, nostrils and mouth.

Sketch in curved lines for the shape of the chest.

Add the outline of the body with long curved lines.

Add long, wavy lines for the hair.

Draw in the legs using the construction lines as a guide.

Draw lines to show the dress fabric hanging loosely on the figure.

Shade areas where light would not reach.

Add straggly lines to create the ragged sleeves and hemline.

Remove any unwanted construction lines.

Draw in the toes.

47

Witch

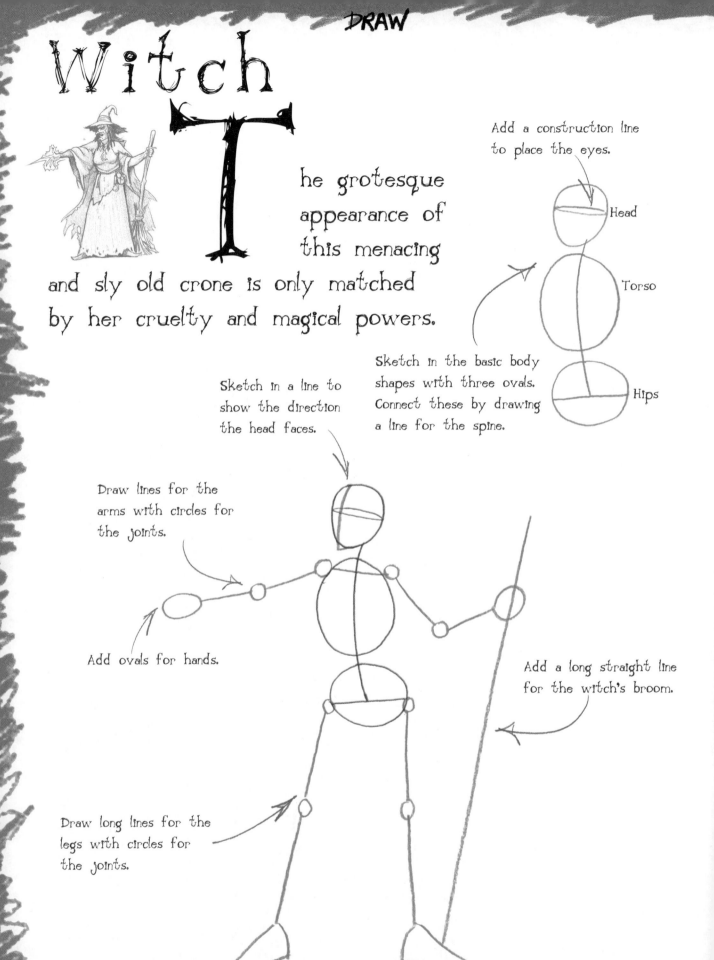

The grotesque appearance of this menacing and sly old crone is only matched by her cruelty and magical powers.

Add a construction line to place the eyes.

Head

Torso

Hips

Sketch in the basic body shapes with three ovals. Connect these by drawing a line for the spine.

Sketch in a line to show the direction the head faces.

Draw lines for the arms with circles for the joints.

Add ovals for hands.

Add a long straight line for the witch's broom.

Draw long lines for the legs with circles for the joints.

Add triangle shapes for the feet.

Draw in the shape of the witch's crooked hat.

Add basic facial features including a long nose!

Draw in the arms using the construction lines as a guide.

Draw this hand grasping the broom.

Add the shape of the broom bristles.

Draw long flaring lines for the clothes.

Complete the details and shading of the crooked hat.

Finish the ugly facial features.

Add ragged edges to her sleeves and clothes.

Draw sharp lines for magic shooting out of the witch's hand.

Add shading to areas where light won't reach.

Add trinkets to the witch's belt.

Add tears and holes to the clothing.

Using an eraser, remove any unwanted construction lines.

49

DRAW
Frankenstein's creature

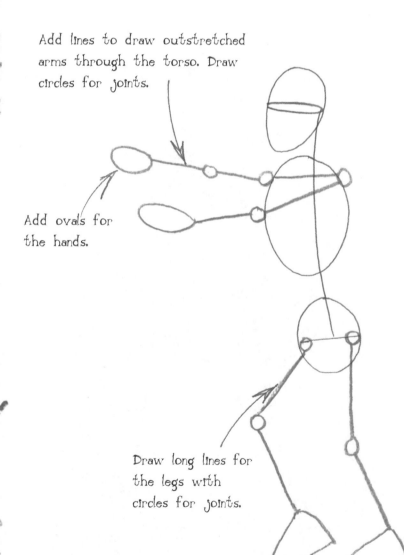

Victor Frankenstein plundered body parts to create an undead being in a terrifying electrical experiment. This man-made creature walks the night alone.

Head

Draw in the position of the eyes

Torso

Hips

Draw two ovals for the head and torso and a circle for the hips. Draw in a centre line and a horizontal line for the hips.

Add lines to draw outstretched arms through the torso. Draw circles for joints.

Add ovals for the hands.

Draw lots of small stick figures to find the best pose. Try posing in front of a mirror to work out what looks best.

Draw long lines for the legs with circles for joints.

Sketch in two triangles for the feet.

Draw fingers on the hands.

Add basic facial features.

Sketch in the hair.

Add a bolt through the neck.

Sketch in the basic shape of the jacket. Make the sleeves look short.

Add a pocket to the jacket.

Draw the trousers and belt using the construction lines as a guide.

Finish the details of the head.

Add some details to the shoes.

Add shading to areas that light won't reach.

Draw patches on the knee and elbow.

Draw the laces and extra detail on the shoes.

Use an eraser to remove any unwanted construction lines.

DRAW
Scarecrow

This frightening character bursts into life at Halloween, scaring innocent bystanders and terrorising nearby towns.

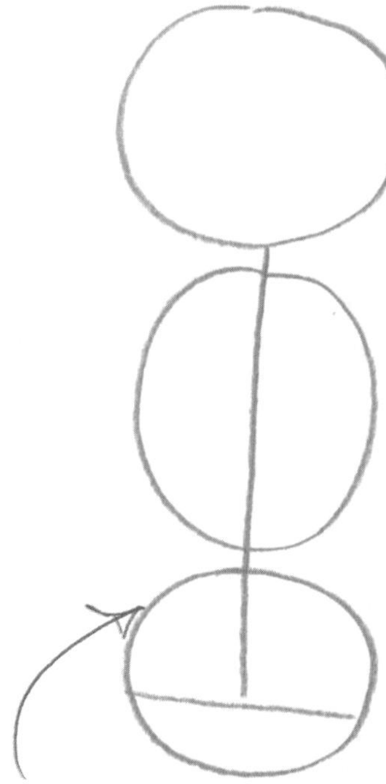

Head

Torso

Hips

Draw two circles for the head and hips and an oval for the torso. Add a curved line for the spine and a horizontal line at the hips.

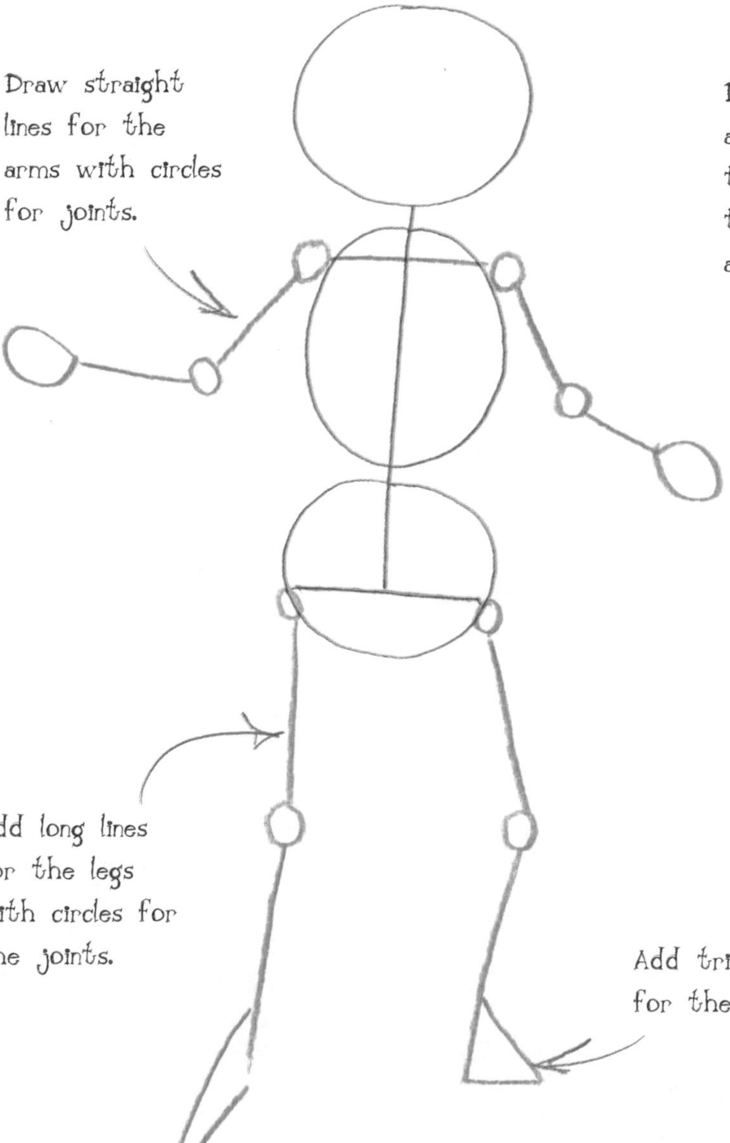

Draw straight lines for the arms with circles for joints.

Add ovals for the hands.

Add long lines for the legs with circles for the joints.

Add triangle shapes for the feet.

52

Draw in the shape of the pumpkin head. Add its scary features.

...w in the branch—like ...pes for the fingers.

Add the shape of the scarf.

Draw in the ragged shape of the coat using the construction lines as a guide.

...raw a ...e—string ...lt.

Add details to the coat, such as tears and patches.

Draw the feet in as spiky branch shapes.

Complete the spiky branch—like hands.

Add shading to areas where light wouldn't reach.

Use jagged lines for the ragged sleeves, trousers and hemlines.

Remove any unwanted construction lines with an eraser.

The Grim Reaper DRAW

Hope you don't meet up with this cloaked figure any time soon! His appearance means your life has come to an end, as he has come to collect your soul.

Head

Torso

Hips

Draw in rounded shapes for the head, neck, torso and hips. Add a line for the spine.

Sketch in the construction lines for the facial features.

Draw a long curved line for the scythe.

Draw straight lines for the arms with circles for the joints.

Add ovals for the hands.

Sketch in long lines for the legs with circles for the joints.

Sketch in the shapes of the feet.

Draw the basic skull features.

Draw the shape of the head inside a loose-fitting hood.

Add curved lines for the blade.

Add the long, open sleeves of the cloak.

Sketch in bony fingers holding the scythe.

Add jagged lines for the flowing edges of the cape and the hemline.

Finish the skull details.

Add lines to create the bony feet.

Complete the details of the scythe.

Add shading to areas where light would not reach.

Draw in a pile of skulls and bones.

Add tonal lines for folds in the cloak.

Use an eraser to remove any unwanted construction lines.

DRAW
Ankylosaurus
(AN–kill–o–sore–us or an–KYLE–o–sore–us)

This herbivore from the Cretaceous period was heavily armoured, which made it almost invulnerable to predators. The club-tipped tail was probably a dangerous weapon.

Draw one large oval for the body of the dinosaur.

Head

Body

Draw a smaller circle for the head.

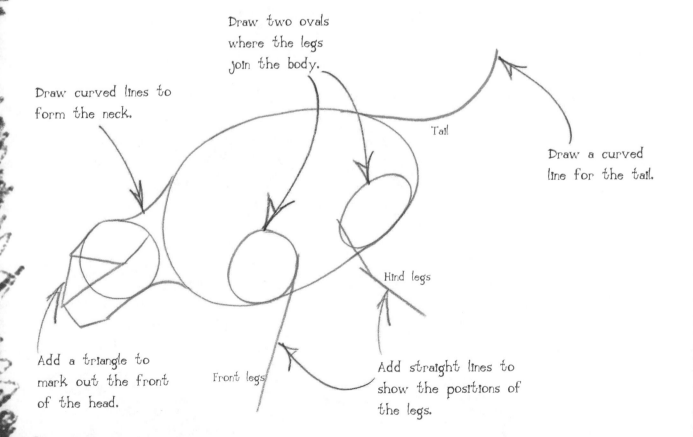

Draw two ovals where the legs join the body.

Draw curved lines to form the neck.

Tail

Draw a curved line for the tail.

Hind legs

Add a triangle to mark out the front of the head.

Front legs

Add straight lines to show the positions of the legs.

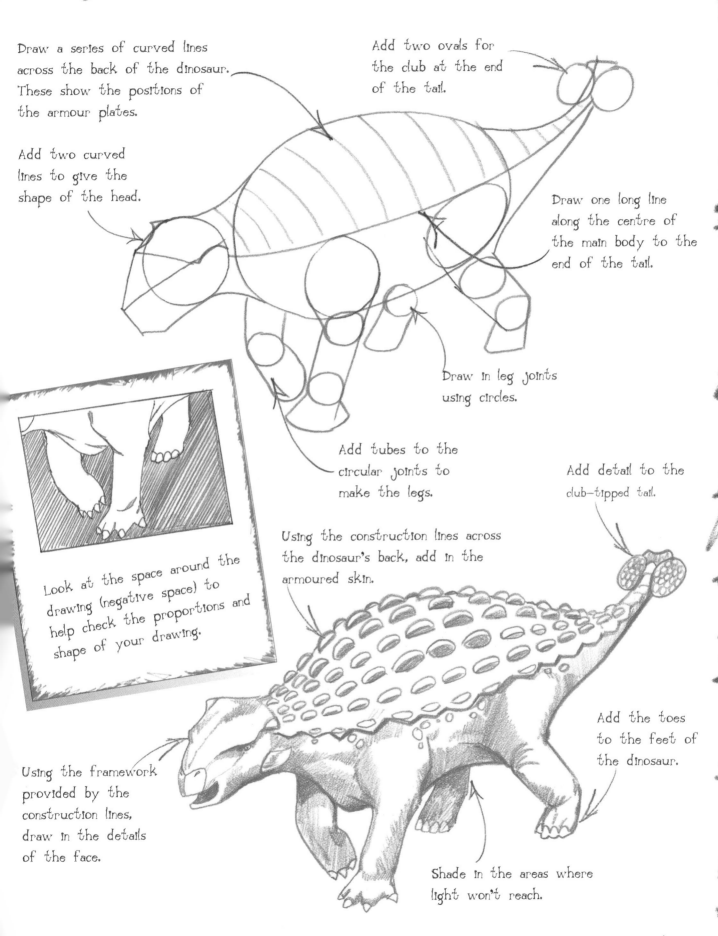

Draw a series of curved lines across the back of the dinosaur. These show the positions of the armour plates.

Add two ovals for the club at the end of the tail.

Add two curved lines to give the shape of the head.

Draw one long line along the centre of the main body to the end of the tail.

Draw in leg joints using circles.

Look at the space around the drawing (negative space) to help check the proportions and shape of your drawing.

Add tubes to the circular joints to make the legs.

Add detail to the club-tipped tail.

Using the construction lines across the dinosaur's back, add in the armoured skin.

Using the framework provided by the construction lines, draw in the details of the face.

Add the toes to the feet of the dinosaur.

Shade in the areas where light won't reach.

57

DRAW
Iguanodon
(ig—WAH—no—don)

Iguanodon was a herbivorous dinosaur that lived in herds and could grow up to 13 metres in length. Its footprints have been found in the rock layers of southern England, Germany and Spain.

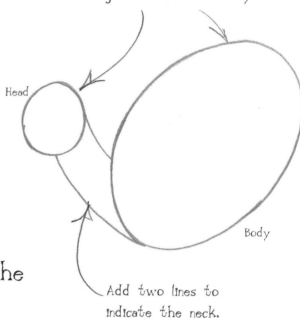

Draw a circle to form the head, and a larger oval for the body.

Head

Body

Add two lines to indicate the neck.

Draw long, straight lines to indicate the hind legs.

Sketch in straight lines for the basic shape of the head.

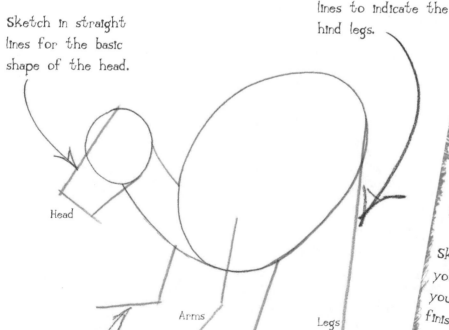

Head

Arms

Legs

Sketch in the position of the arms using straight lines.

Sketching in construction lines helps you create and keep the shape of your drawing. Once the drawing is finished, remove any that are left.

Using the construction line as the centre, draw a triangle and a semicircle to complete the shape of the head.

Add two curving lines for the shape of the tail.

Sketch in the joints of each limb using circles.

Sketch in the positions of the hands using a combination of rectangles and triangles.

For the feet, draw two straight lines coming off the joint at an angle, then join them using a curved line.

Add lines to create the shape of the legs.

Add skin detail.

Draw in the eyes and mouth, shading the areas away from the light to give it shape.

Small sketched lines can make the skin look textured.

Add the fingers and claws.

Using the construction lines for the shape, complete the feet of the Iguanodon.

59

Liopleurodon

(lee-o-PLOO-ro-don)

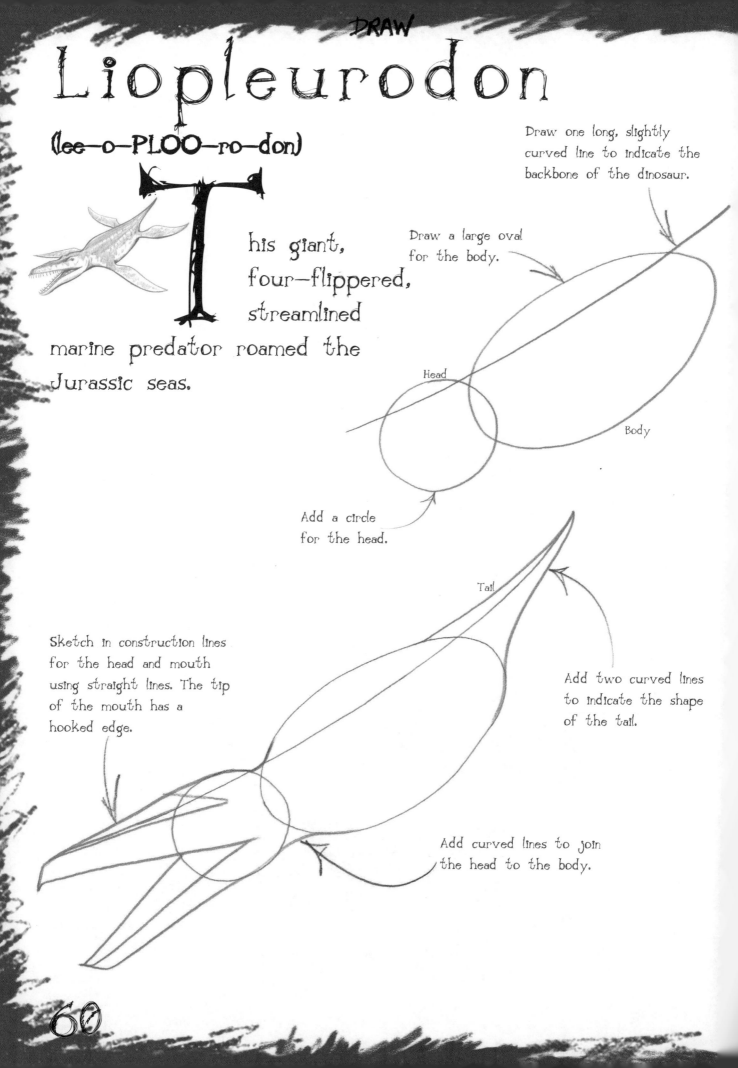

This giant, four-flippered, streamlined marine predator roamed the Jurassic seas.

Draw one long, slightly curved line to indicate the backbone of the dinosaur.

Draw a large oval for the body.

Head

Body

Add a circle for the head.

Tail

Sketch in construction lines for the head and mouth using straight lines. The tip of the mouth has a hooked edge.

Add two curved lines to indicate the shape of the tail.

Add curved lines to join the head to the body.

Add the fins on this side with a series of three simple curved lines.

Fin

Indicate the position of the eye.

The fins on the near side are drawn with three simple curved lines, joined to the body with small ovals.

Sketch in the shape of the tongue using two curved lines.

Using an eraser (rubber), highlight lines down the back of the Liopleurodon to give it shape.

Add shading to the back of the creature.

Finish the details of the eye.

Add shading for the skin texture.

Add the sharp teeth of the Liopleurodon.

61

DRAW

Parasaurolophus
(para–saw–ROL–o–fus)

This was one of the 'duck–billed' dinosaurs. Its hollow, bony crest was longer than the rest of its skull, and may have been used to produce a foghorn–like sound.

Draw a circle for the head.

Head

Neck

Draw two large ovals for the main body.

Add two lines for the neck.

Join the ovals with two lines.

Sketch three straight lines to show the shape of the head.

Head

Draw a long, curved line to indicate the position of the tail.

Tail

Hold your picture up to a mirror to look at it in reverse. This will really help you to see any mistakes.

Arms

The front arms are drawn with a series of small circles for the joints; join these with straight lines.

Legs

Sketch in the construction lines for the hind legs, using a series of straight lines with circles for the joints.

Use curved lines to complete the back of the head.

Sketch in the mouth, eye and curved neck, using your construction lines as a guide.

Sketch in the shape of the hands with short, straight lines.

Draw two straight lines on the bottom of the foot, adding semicircles to show the toes.

Add another curved line to complete the tail.

Use the construction lines to help you finish the eye and mouth.

Complete the detail on the head.

Gently shade in the back of the dinosaur to show the texture of the skin.

inish the hands, adding hade on the underside f the arms.

dd the detail on the eet, shading darker areas n the curve of the toes.

Shade the underside of the body where light won't reach.

63

DRAW Pteranodon
(te-RAN-o-don)

The Pteranodon flew on huge wings of stretched skin. It was alive during the Cretaceous period. Its crest was presumably used for display.

First draw a simple cross.

Draw two circles for the head and body of the Pteranodon.

Head

Body

Sketch in the bottom half of the body using curved lines.

Sketch in the position of the head with three simple lines.

Draw a single curved line through the body of the Pteranodon for the arms.

Head

Arm

Wing

Add long, curved lines to show the top edge of the wings.

Leg

Sketch two curved lines coming down off the body of the Pteranodon to show the positions of the legs.

64

Lightly sketch in the basic shape of the hands.

Draw in the eye.

Add a curved line to the rear of the head to complete the shape of the skull.

Hand

Sketch in the triangular shape of the mouth.

Sketch in the underside of the arm.

Add two long, curved lines for the bottom edge of the wings.

Add another curved line to finish the shape of the legs.

Sketch in the shape of the feet.

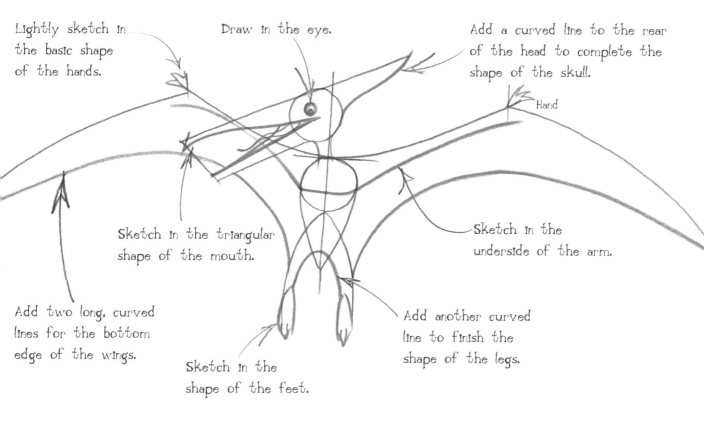

Shade the underside of the wing.

Finish the detail on the head, shading areas to give it shape.

Draw in the hands with sharp claws.

Using the construction lines, finish the mouth, adding a tongue and very dark areas inside the mouth.

The darkest areas of shade will be where the wing meets the body.

Finish the feet, making sure they end in sharp points for the talons.

65

Styracosaurus

(sty—RACK—o—sore—us)

Styracosaurus ('spiked lizard') was alive during the Cretaceous period. It had up to nine horns and spikes around its neck to help it in fights, and weighed about 3 tonnes.

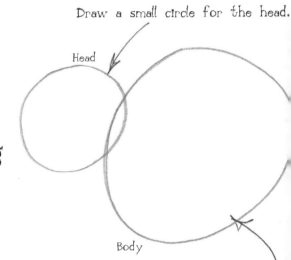

Draw a small circle for the head.

Head

Body

Draw a large circle for the body.

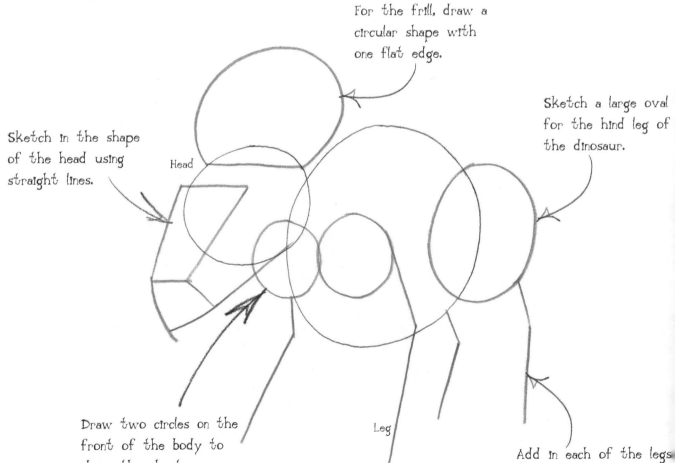

For the frill, draw a circular shape with one flat edge.

Sketch a large oval for the hind leg of the dinosaur.

Sketch in the shape of the head using straight lines.

Head

Draw two circles on the front of the body to show the chest.

Leg

Add in each of the legs with straight lines.

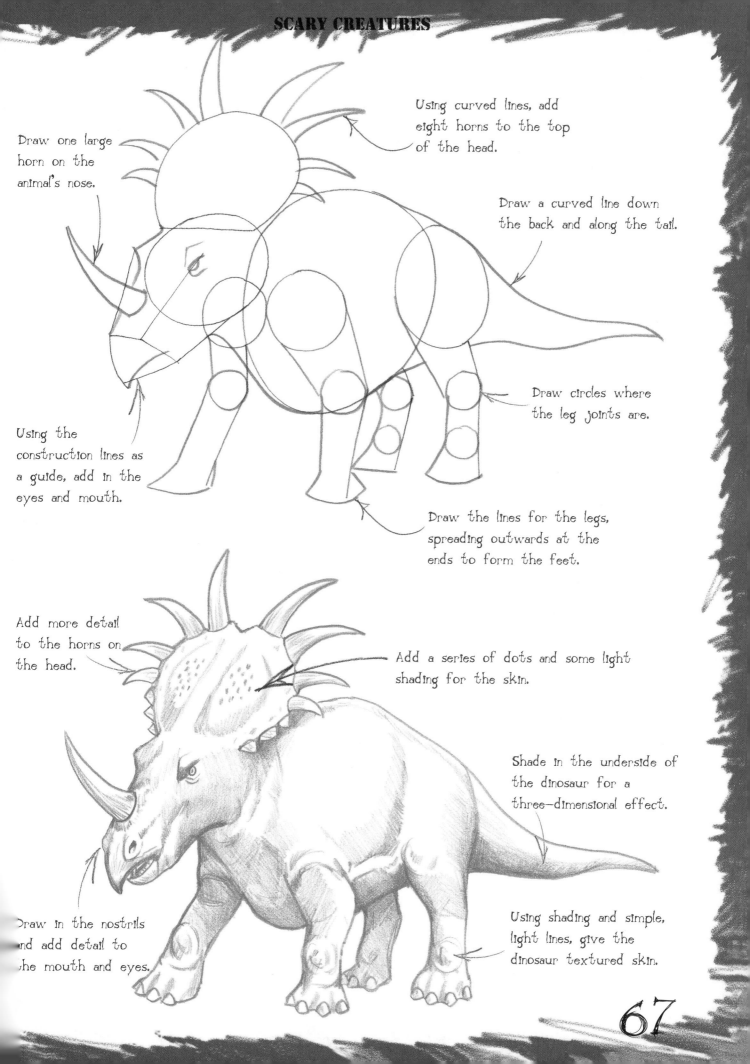

Draw one large
horn on the
animal's nose.

Using curved lines, add
eight horns to the top
of the head.

Draw a curved line down
the back and along the tail.

Draw circles where
the leg joints are.

Using the
construction lines as
a guide, add in the
eyes and mouth.

Draw the lines for the legs,
spreading outwards at the
ends to form the feet.

Add more detail
to the horns on
the head.

Add a series of dots and some light
shading for the skin.

Shade in the underside of
the dinosaur for a
three-dimensional effect.

Draw in the nostrils
and add detail to
the mouth and eyes.

Using shading and simple,
light lines, give the
dinosaur textured skin.

67

Stegosaurus

(steg–o–SORE–us)

Stegosaurus ('plated lizard') was a herbivore alive in the Jurassic period, 140 million years ago. It had large plates that ran down its spine from neck to tail. Its tail also had spikes on it for defence, that were nearly a metre long.

Sketch a large oval for the body.

Body

Head

Draw a small circle for the head and connect it to the body with curved lines to show the neck.

Draw in the top of the leg with a large circle.

Sketch the dinosaur's head with three simple lines.

Neck

Draw in the tail from the rear of the body using two curved lines.

Tail

Foot

Leg

Each foot of the Stegosaurus can be sketched in using simple semicircles.

Use circles for the knee joints, and join these to the feet with straight lines.

Draw two curved construction lines to help you draw in the plates on the dinosaur's back.

Each plate is drawn with four simple lines. Your curved construction lines (one for each row of plates) will help you judge how large they should be.

Sketch in the eyes and mouth.

Draw four straight lines coming out of the tail for the spikes.

Draw the second row of plates behind the first, again using the construction lines to judge their size.

Add detail to each plate with small lines and shading.

Shade the underside of the dinosaur to give a three-dimensional effect.

Finish drawing the eyes and mouth.

Finish the spikes on the tail by adding curved lines coming to a point at the end.

DRAW
Brachiosaurus
(brack—ee—o—SORE—us)

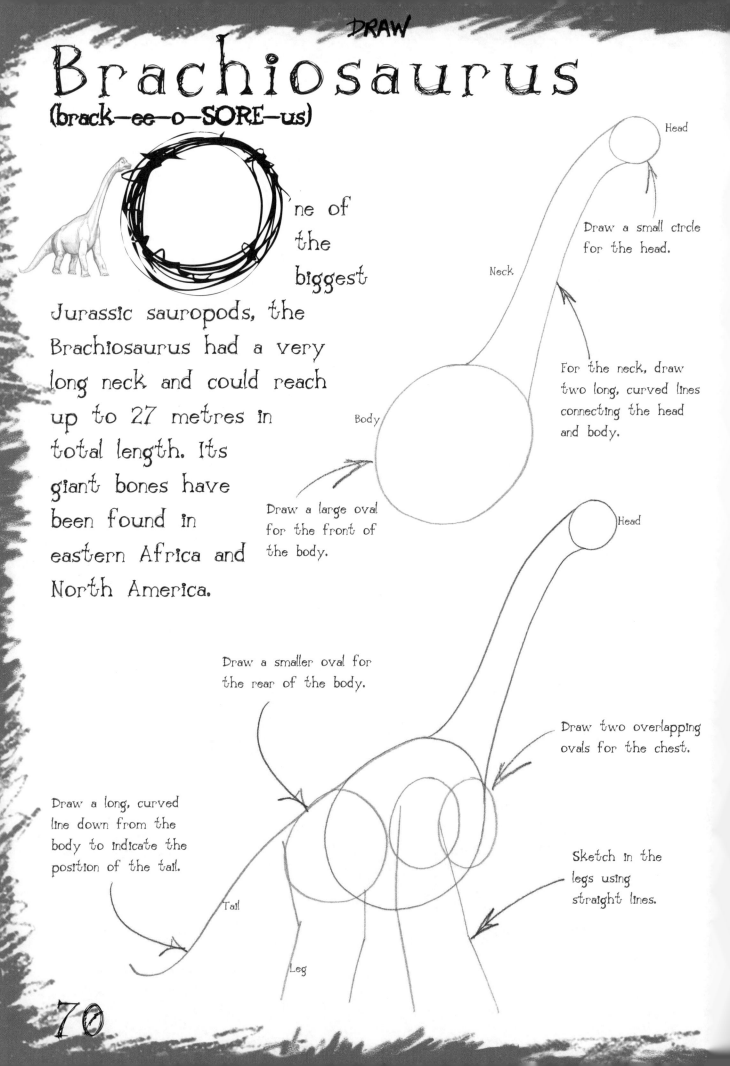

One of the biggest Jurassic sauropods, the Brachiosaurus had a very long neck and could reach up to 27 metres in total length. Its giant bones have been found in eastern Africa and North America.

Head

Draw a small circle for the head.

Neck

For the neck, draw two long, curved lines connecting the head and body.

Body

Draw a large oval for the front of the body.

Head

Draw a smaller oval for the rear of the body.

Draw two overlapping ovals for the chest.

Draw a long, curved line down from the body to indicate the position of the tail.

Sketch in the legs using straight lines.

Tail

Leg

Using squares or rectangles to frame your drawing can make it look completely different.

Draw in the construction lines of the mouth, eye and top of the head.

Finish constructing the legs with straight lines.

Mark in the joints with circles.

Add the detail to the head, including teeth, and shading to give it shape.

Draw in the underside of the tail with a long, curved line similar to the top of the tail.

Sketch in the feet using semicircles.

Use sketchy lines to give texture to the skin of the dinosaur.

Add shading, paying attention to where the joints are shown in your construction lines.

Shade in the areas where light would not reach.

Draw in the toes on each foot.

71

DRAW
Velociraptor
(ve-LOSS-e-rap-tor)

The Velociraptor ('swift robber') lived 85 million years ago during the Cretaceous period. It was one of the fastest dinosaurs, moving at around 65 kph!

Draw a circle for the head.

Head

Neck

Body

Join the head and body with two curved lines for the neck.

Draw a larger oval for the body.

Add a long, curved line for the tail.

Tail

Draw in the thigh of the Velociraptor with a narrow oval.

Draw a triangle and add construction lines to form a wedge shape for the front of the Velociraptor's head.

Add another, smaller, narrow oval for the further leg.

Leg

Sketch in the shape of the lower part of the legs with a series of curved lines.

Add a long, curved line for the underside of the tail, continuing it to complete the underside of the body.

Use the wedge-shaped construction lines to sketch in the face.

Each arm is made up of three circular joints, joined up with simple lines.

Sketch in the shape of the toes.

Talon

Add talons to the ends of the toes.

Complete the head, drawing the detail of the eyes and adding teeth.

Add shading along the back of the Velociraptor.

Use your oval construction lines to draw the shape of the thigh and leg.

Using the construction lines, complete the hands, adding three talons to each.

Small lines can be added to give texture, such as wrinkles, to the skin.

Add shading and detail to the feet.

73

Tyrannosaurus rex

(tie-RAN-o-sore-us REX)

At 5 tonnes and 12 metres in length, Tyrannosaurus rex ('tyrant lizard king') was one of the biggest theropods of all time. It was alive 85 million years ago in the Cretaceous period. The massive jaws and teeth provided an awesome biting force.

Above the body, draw a circle for the head, and two lines to form the neck. The line for the rear of the neck should miss the head slightly, then curve in.

Head

Neck

Body

Draw a large oval for the body.

Sketch in the construction lines for the head.

Position the arms by drawing ovals for the chest and a circle for the beginning of each arm.

Draw in the tail using two curved lines joining at the tip.

Tail

Draw a line from the chest down to the legs to complete the body shape.

Draw a narrow oval for the top of the hind leg.

Legs

Sketch in the legs using straight lines.

Using the construction lines, draw in the main details of the head. Include the nostrils, mouth and teeth.

Use the construction line midway through the head to mark the top of the mouth.

Draw circles on the construction lines for the elbow and wrist, joining them with straight lines.

The hand is a basic shape consisting of four lines.

Add a circle for the lower joint of the knee.

Use straight lines to complete the legs, with three pointed toes.

Use the construction lines to help you define the shape of the dinosaur's body.

Complete the detail on the head.

Add dark shading to the back for a chiaroscuro effect.

Draw many lines on the dinosaur's skin to give it texture.

The use of light and dark to create bold images is called chiaroscuro. Try this on your dinosaur to get more impact.

Finish the details of the feet, adding talons.

75

Centaur

A centaur is half horse, half man. Centaurs were said to have come from the mountains of Thessaly in Greece, and were wild, lawless and savage. The Greek hero Heracles killed centaurs with poison—tipped arrows.

Draw in a rectangle for the centaur's chest.

Man body

Draw two circles to form the body.

Draw in centre line

Draw in lines for the back and the belly.

Horse bo[dy]

Draw the ground the centaur stands on.

Draw a line for the spear.

Head

Spear

Draw a small circle for a head and two lines to form a neck.

Arm

Front legs

Back legs

Add lines for the legs and arms, with circles for the joints, hands and hooves.

76

Indicate the positions of the eyes, nose and mouth.

Add hair to the centaur's head.

Draw in the muscles of the upper body.

Draw in the muscles of the lower body, and curved lines to show the position of the tail.

Add detail to the centaur's hands.

Draw in the detail of the spear.

Finish drawing in the eyes, nose and mouth.

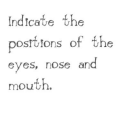

Use squares or rectangles to frame your composition. This can make all the difference.

Shade in the muscles.

Pencil lines should follow the direction of the tail.

Take a look at real horses' legs.

77

Crouching dragon

DRAW

Dragons are thought to have magical and spiritual powers, and are common to many cultures of the world. These cunning creatures typically have scaly bodies, wings and fiery breath. The Chinese consider them symbols of good luck.

Draw a circle to form the head, and a larger oval for the main body.

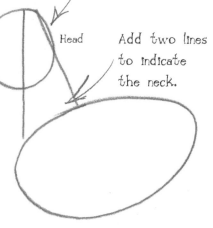

Head

Add two lines to indicate the neck.

Main body

Sketch in shapes for the top of the head and the lower jaw.

Draw in lines for the wing base and circles for the joints.

Add a long curved line to show the position of the tail.

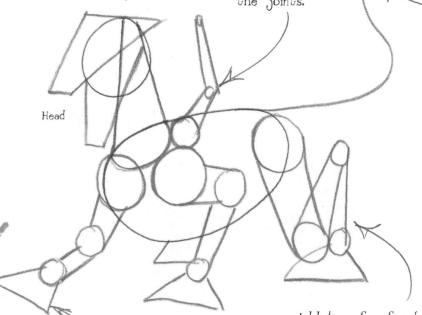

Head

Try some chiaroscuro (bold contrast of light and dark) to give your dragon more impact.

Add lines for front and rear legs, with circles for the joints.

Draw triangular shapes to indicate the positions of the feet.

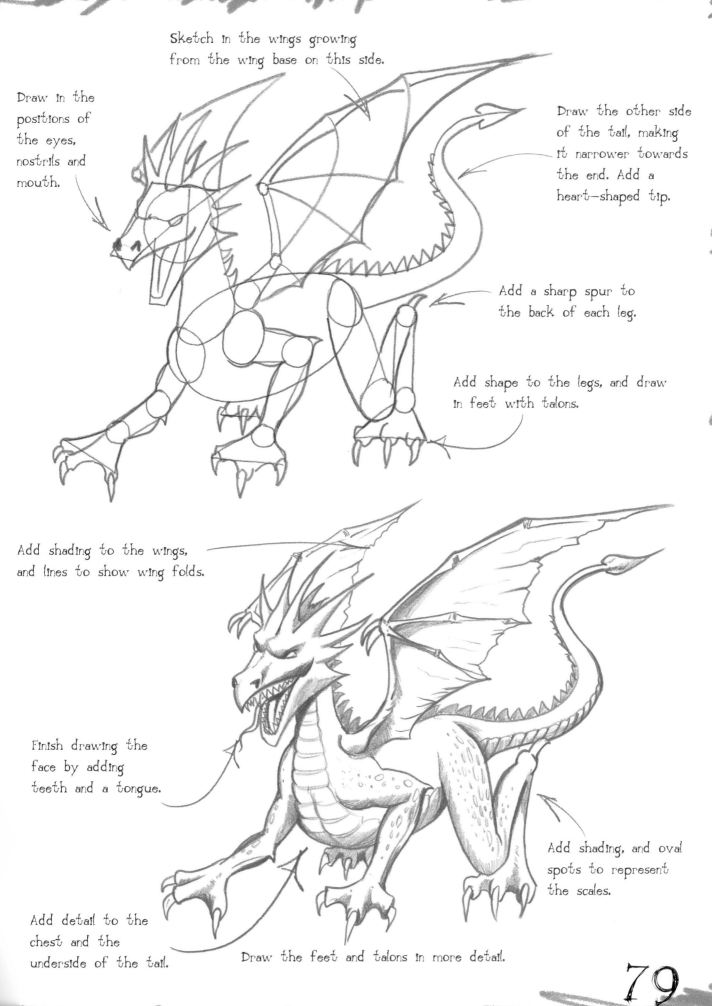

Sketch in the wings growing from the wing base on this side.

Draw in the positions of the eyes, nostrils and mouth.

Draw the other side of the tail, making it narrower towards the end. Add a heart-shaped tip.

Add a sharp spur to the back of each leg.

Add shape to the legs, and draw in feet with talons.

Add shading to the wings, and lines to show wing folds.

Finish drawing the face by adding teeth and a tongue.

Add shading, and oval spots to represent the scales.

Add detail to the chest and the underside of the tail.

Draw the feet and talons in more detail.

79

Gryphon

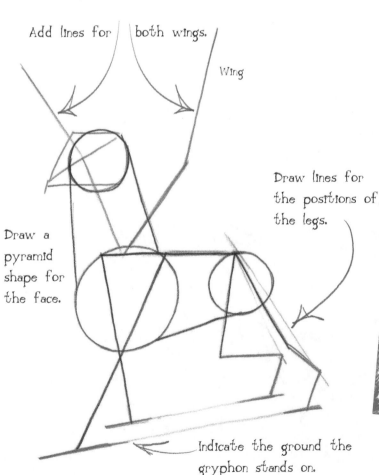

The gryphon (griffin) or lion—eagle was considered to be the king of the air, and was a powerful and majestic creature. In Persian culture, gryphons are shown drawing the sun across the sky.

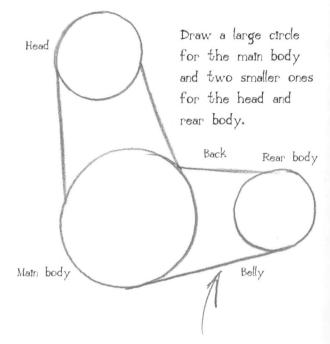

Head

Back   Rear body

Main body   Belly

Draw a large circle for the main body and two smaller ones for the head and rear body.

Draw in lines for the neck and for the back and belly.

Add lines for   both wings.

Wing

Draw a pyramid shape for the face.

Draw lines for the positions of the legs.

Indicate the ground the gryphon stands on.

Look at the space around the figure (negative space) to help check the proportions and shape of your drawing.

Wing construction

First draw two straight lines.

Add two oval shapes.

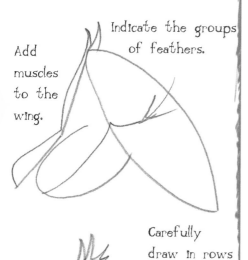

Add muscles to the wing.

Indicate the groups of feathers.

Carefully draw in rows of feathers.

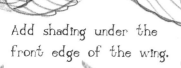

Add shading under the front edge of the wing.

Carefully sketch in the beak, then add ears and eyes.

Draw in a shield-like shape at the base of the body.

Add a curved, lion-like tail.

Add details of back feet and legs.

Sketch in the front feet.

Finish drawing the detail of the gryphon's head.

Use short downward strokes to draw the chest feathers.

Add wing features (see left).

Add shading.

Draw the sharp eagle's talons.

Add hair to the tip of the tail.

Hydra

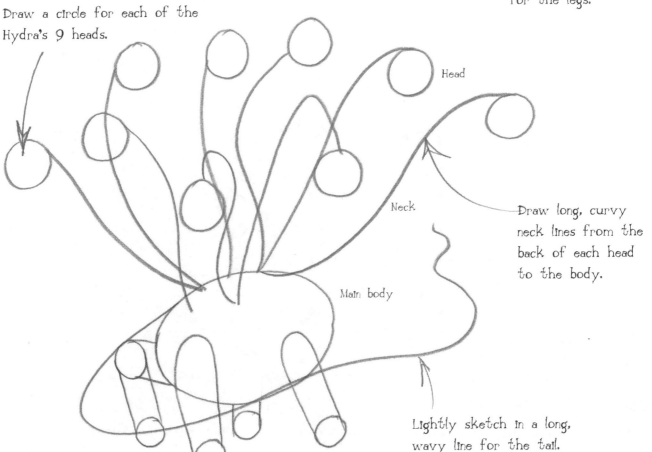

The Hydra in Greek mythology was said to guard the entrance to the underworld beneath the waters of Lake Lerna. Heracles killed this hideous creature as one of his twelve labours.

Add two lines to join this leg to the body.

Draw a large oval for the main body.

Main body

Legs

Draw four tube shapes for the legs.

Draw a circle for each of the Hydra's 9 heads.

Head

Neck

Draw long, curvy neck lines from the back of each head to the body.

Main body

Lightly sketch in a long, wavy line for the tail.

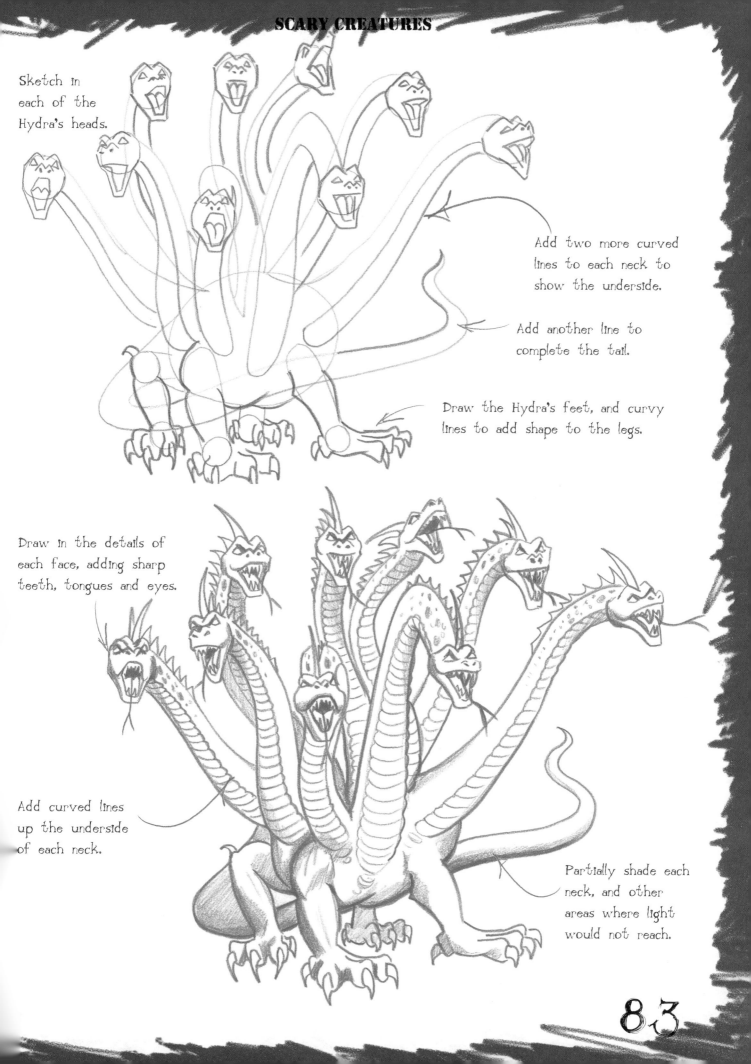

Sketch in each of the Hydra's heads.

Add two more curved lines to each neck to show the underside.

Add another line to complete the tail.

Draw the Hydra's feet, and curvy lines to add shape to the legs.

Draw in the details of each face, adding sharp teeth, tongues and eyes.

Add curved lines up the underside of each neck.

Partially shade each neck, and other areas where light would not reach.

Minotaur

The Minotaur was half man, half bull. This creature of Greek myth was said to dwell in the labyrinth constructed for King Minos at Knossos. Theseus eventually killed the beast, then found his way out safely by following the trail of string he had left to guide him.

Draw a vertical line through the centre.

Sketch in two circles and an oval to form the head, main body and hips.

Head

Main body

Hips

Centre line

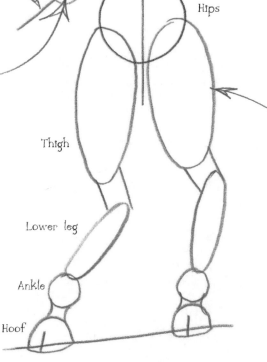

Centre line

Head

Draw a line to indicate the top of the shoulders.

Arms

Sketch two ovals, one smaller and overlapping the other, to show the right arm bent at the elbow. Add a circle for the hand.

Draw a straight line passing through the hand shapes for the axe haft.

Hips

Sketch a long oval shape with a roundish oval below it to show the foreshortening of the left arm. Add a smaller overlapping circle for the hand.

Thigh

Lower leg

Draw a large oval for each thigh. Add two lines to join these to smaller ovals which form the lower legs. Add circles at the end of each leg for ankles, and sketch in the hooves with two semicircles.

Ankle

Hoof

84

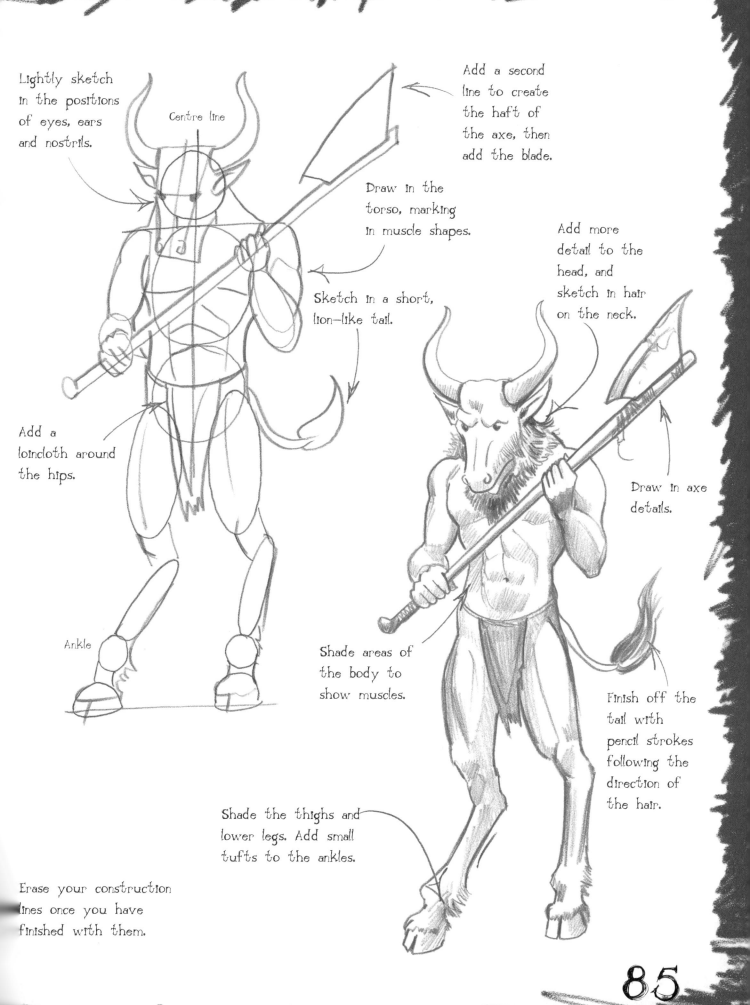

Lightly sketch in the positions of eyes, ears and nostrils.

Centre line

Add a second line to create the haft of the axe, then add the blade.

Draw in the torso, marking in muscle shapes.

Add more detail to the head, and sketch in hair on the neck.

Sketch in a short, lion-like tail.

Add a loincloth around the hips.

Draw in axe details.

Ankle

Shade areas of the body to show muscles.

Finish off the tail with pencil strokes following the direction of the hair.

Shade the thighs and lower legs. Add small tufts to the ankles.

Erase your construction lines once you have finished with them.

Phoenix

The phoenix is a mythical bird said to live for up to 1,461 years. It has red and gold plumage. Each time it nears the end of its life, the phoenix builds a nest of cinnamon twigs that ignites. Both the bird and its nest are turned into ashes, from which a new phoenix arises.

Draw a vertical line to mark the centre of the phoenix.

Sketch a small circle for the head.

Draw a large oval for the body.

Draw two curved lines almost parallel for the neck.

Draw thin legs splayed outwards. The tops of the legs look like short trousers.

Draw a triangular-shaped top beak. Add a lower part.

Indicate the position of the eye.

Lightly sketch in the wing shape and guidelines for the feathers.

Sketch fan-shaped tail feathers.

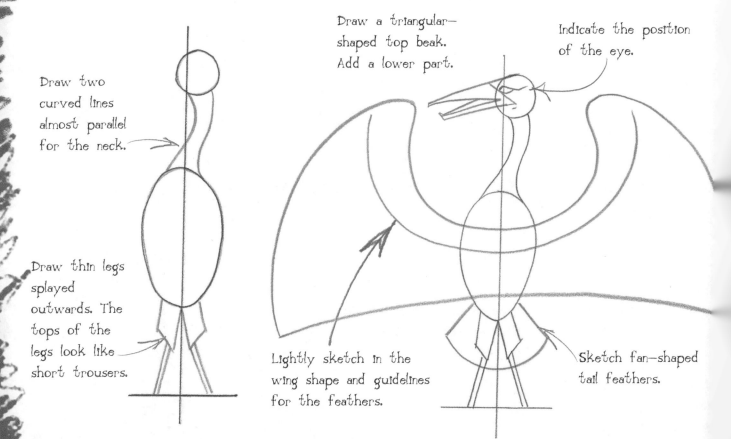

Add a plume of feathers to the back of the head.

Draw in the large lower feathers.

Carefully sketch in the front of the wings.

Sketch in a blazing nest beneath the phoenix.

Draw in the feet with an egg resting between them.

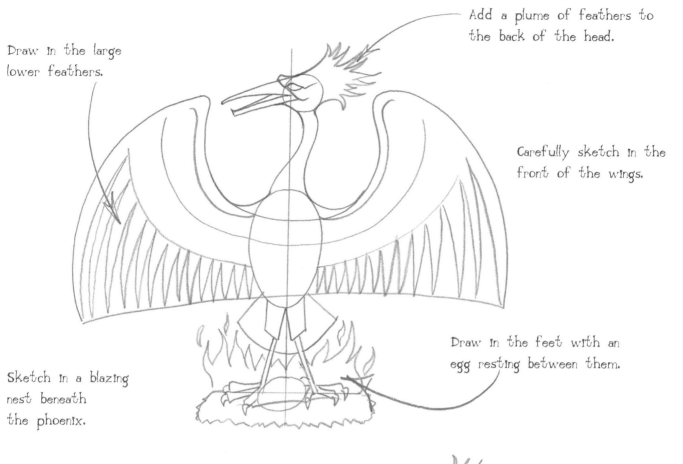

Draw two more rows of feathers on the wings.

Flames

Draw in zigzag lines to give the effect of feathers on the main body.

Remove any unwanted construction lines.

87

Troll

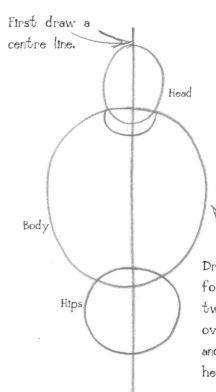

The large mountain troll features in many folk tales. They are said to be foul-smelling creatures that are dim-witted but powerful. Trolls are aggressive towards humans and carry a crude, primitive club as a weapon.

First draw a centre line.

Head

Body

Hips

Draw a large circle for the body. Draw two smaller circles overlapping at top and bottom for the head and hips.

Sketch in a series of overlapping ovals to show the foreshortening of the arms.

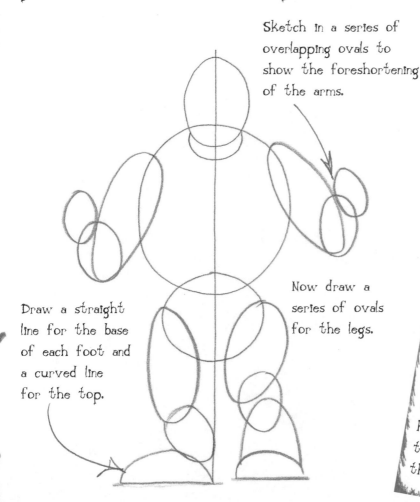

Now draw a series of ovals for the legs.

Draw a straight line for the base of each foot and a curved line for the top.

To draw the face, first draw a line down the centre of the head, then two horizontal lines to help you construct the face. The top horizontal line shows the position of the eyes, the top of the nose and where the ears join the head. The bottom horizontal line shows the base of the nose and the bottom of the ears.

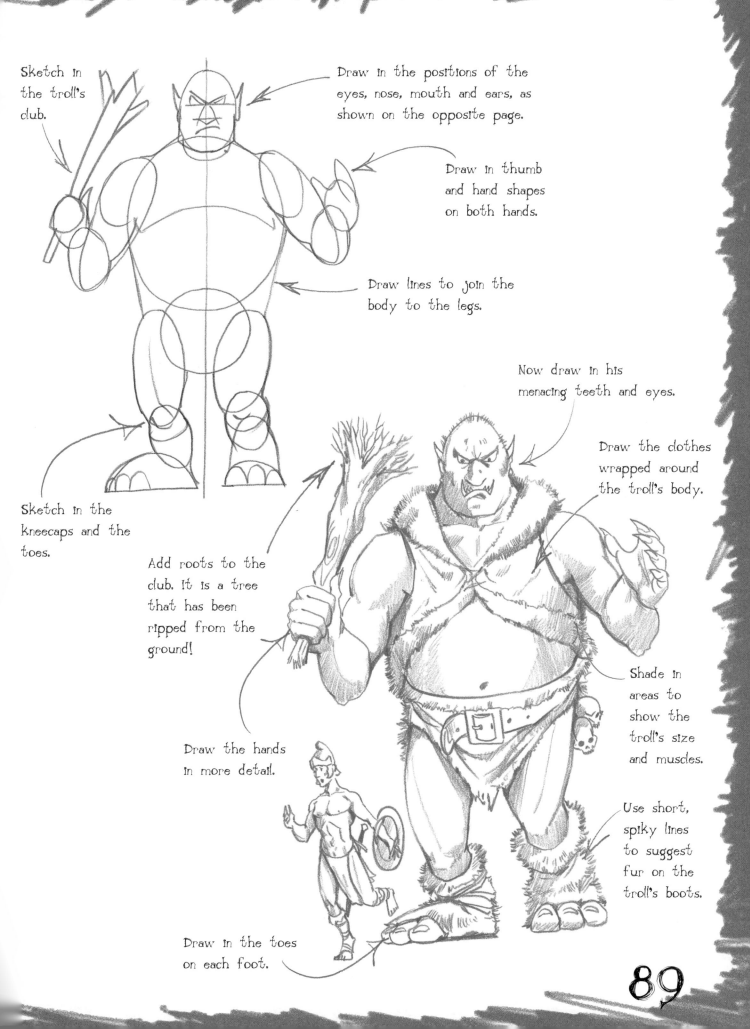

Sketch in the troll's club.

Draw in the positions of the eyes, nose, mouth and ears, as shown on the opposite page.

Draw in thumb and hand shapes on both hands.

Draw lines to join the body to the legs.

Now draw in his menacing teeth and eyes.

Draw the clothes wrapped around the troll's body.

Sketch in the kneecaps and the toes.

Add roots to the club. It is a tree that has been ripped from the ground!

Shade in areas to show the troll's size and muscles.

Draw the hands in more detail.

Use short, spiky lines to suggest fur on the troll's boots.

Draw in the toes on each foot.

89

Tiger's head DRAW

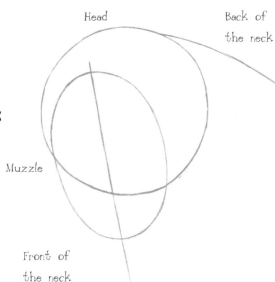

An average male tiger stands 90 cm tall at shoulder height. Unlike other members of the cat family, tigers are not good tree climbers. However, they are strong swimmers and in floods they are known to swim in search of stranded prey.

Draw a circle for the head and an oval for the muzzle.

Head

Back of the neck

Muzzle

Front of the neck

Add lines for the front and back of the neck.

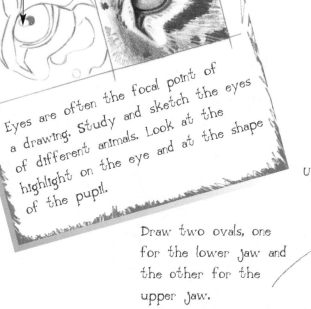

Eyes are often the focal point of a drawing. Study and sketch the eyes of different animals. Look at the highlight on the eye and at the shape of the pupil.

Highlight

Shadow

Look carefully at the angle of the ears and draw them in. Indicate the eye position.

Ear

Ear

Upper jaw

Lower jaw

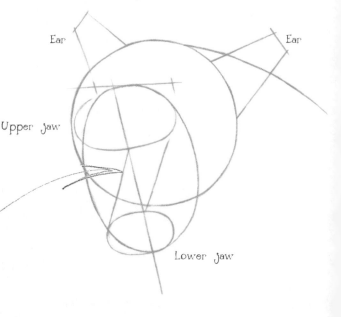

Draw two ovals, one for the lower jaw and the other for the upper jaw.

Draw two lines to join the lower jaw to the back of the mouth.

The maximum lifespan of a tiger is usually around 26 years and for most of their lives, tigers live alone.

Draw in the fur on either side of the face.

Draw in the large front teeth (top and bottom).

Draw the tiger's gums and the position of its back teeth.

Draw the screwed-up face and eyes of the tiger.

Sketch in the shape of the tiger's stripes. Block in the areas of grey tone first, and then the areas of dark tone.

Lastly, use a fine brush and white paint for the paler whiskers.

Lion

The magnificent lion is the second largest of the big cats. Fully grown males can weigh over 230 kg and can measure over 3 m long from tail tip to nose. A lion's roar can be heard up to 8 km away and is the loudest sound made by any big cat.

Draw circles for the head, muzzle and rear and a large oval for the front of the body.

Head

Rear

Muzzle

Belly

Front

Draw lines under the belly and up to the muzzle.

Use the size of the lion's head as a unit of measurement to help keep your drawing in proportion. The lion is 3 heads tall and its body is 3.5 heads long.

Mark out the eye line and the sides of the muzzle.

Back

Mane

Add lines for the position of the legs and the lion's feet. Draw lines for the back and tail.

Tail

Legs

Sketch in circles for the lion's mane and ears.

Draw a curved line to show the high arch of the lion's back.

Lightly draw in the shape of the eyes, nose and mouth.

Extend the line of the mane down to its belly.

Sketch in the front of the legs and the lion's paws.

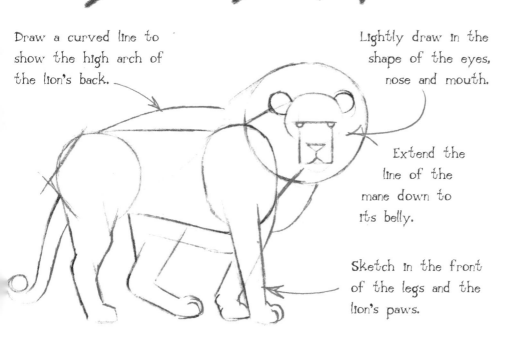

Make the lion's hindquarters more angular.

Finish drawing the hindquarters. Shade in the muscles.

Draw the lion's mane, using your pencil marks to follow the direction of the hair.

Finish drawing in the eyes, nose and mouth.

A mane can make a lion appear larger, which scares away other male lions.

93

Glossary

Chiaroscuro The practice of drawing high-contrast pictures with a lot of black and white, but not much grey.

Composition The arrangement of the parts of a picture on the drawing paper.

Construction lines Guidelines used in the early stages of a drawing. They are usually erased later.

Cretaceous The period from 146 to 65 million years ago. Dinosaurs died out at the end of this period.

Fixative A type of resin used to spray over a finished drawing to prevent smudging. **It should only be used by an adult.**

Focal point A central point of interest.

Foreshortening Drawing part of a figure shorter than it really is, so it looks as though it is pointing towards the viewer.

Jurassic The period from 200 to 146 million years ago, when many kinds of dinosaurs lived.

Light source The direction from which the light seems to come in a drawing.

Perspective A method of drawing in which near objects are shown larger than faraway objects to give an impression of depth.

Pose The position assumed by a figure.

Proportion The correct relationship of scale between each part of the drawing.

Silhouette A drawing that shows only a flat, dark shape, like a shadow.

Three-dimensional Having an effect of depth, so as to look lifelike or real.

Vanishing point The place in a perspective drawing where parallel lines appear to meet.

Index